AF338297

Fun Fan Facts:

The Unofficial World Cup Edition

Group H

Spain, Cabo Verde, Saudi Arabia & Uruguay

Everything Young Fans Should Know

By: Jake Liam

Fun Fan Facts: The Unofficial World Cup Edition - Group H

Dedication

To the fans of Group H, where history, heart, and hunger all collide.

From Spain's beautiful style, to Cabo Verde's fearless spirit, to Saudi Arabia's growing confidence, and Uruguay's never-quit mentality, this group is full of teams ready to make their moment count.

Four teams. One stage. Endless possibility.

Because in Group H, every whistle could start something unforgettable.

Introduction

Welcome, fans! Whether you are brand new to the World Cup or you have been following every match for years, this book has everything you need to know about the four teams in Group H. Get ready to impress your friends with facts, history, and highlights from Spain, Cabo Verde, Saudi Arabia, and Uruguay as they battle it out on the biggest stage in football!

Quick Timeout

This book is packed with facts. Like, A LOT of facts. Every fact was checked, double-checked, and triple-checked. But here is the thing about football history: not everyone agrees on everything.

In the United States, this game is usually called soccer. Almost everywhere else, it is called football. Same sport. Same ball. Same goals.

In this book, we will use both. No rules broken. No arguments needed. Nobody is getting a yellow card at the dinner table. One thing stays the same: this game is loved all over the world.

HOW IT WORKS

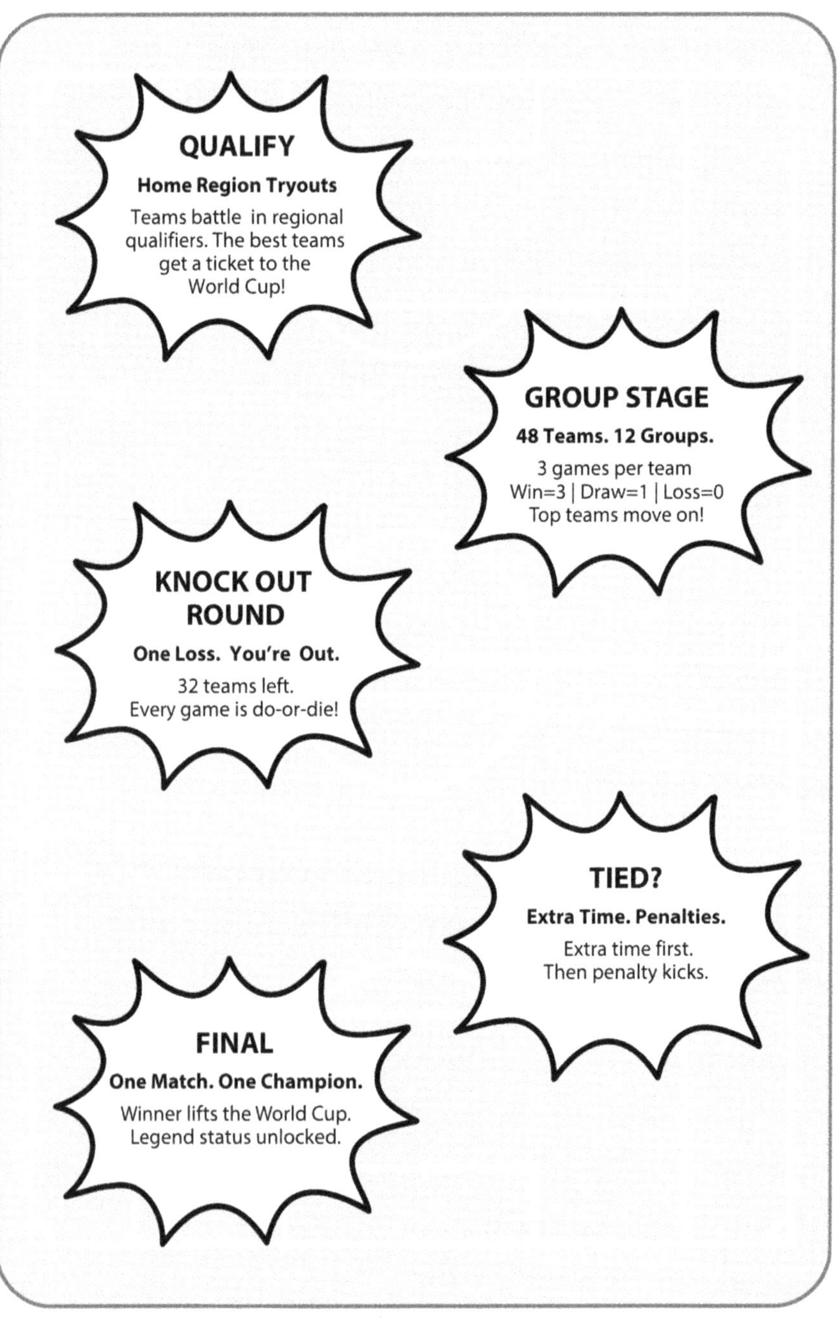

QUALIFY
Home Region Tryouts
Teams battle in regional qualifiers. The best teams get a ticket to the World Cup!
GROUP STAGE
48 Teams. 12 Groups.
3 games per team
Win=3 | Draw=1 | Loss=0
Top teams move on!
KNOCK OUT ROUND
One Loss. You're Out.
32 teams left.
Every game is do-or-die!
TIED?
Extra Time. Penalties.
Extra time first.
Then penalty kicks.
FINAL
One Match. One Champion.
Winner lifts the World Cup.
Legend status unlocked.

How the World Cup Works

The World Cup is the biggest soccer tournament on Earth. When it starts, the entire planet pays attention. It happens every four years. In 2026, it gets extra wild because three countries host it: Mexico, Canada, and the USA. There will be 48 teams. That is a lot of jerseys.

How Teams Get There

Before the World Cup, teams play qualifying games in their own part of the world (like Europe, Africa, Asia, and South America). The best teams earn a spot in the World Cup. It is basically soccer's giant tryout, without any orange slices at halftime.

Step 1: The Group Stage

The 48 teams are split into 12 lettered groups of 4 teams. Each team plays 3 games, one against each team in their group. Each game lasts 90 minutes, with two 45-minute halves.

Points are easy:

- Win get 3 points
- Draw get 1 point each
- Lose get 0 points

After the group games, the top 2 teams from each group move on. The 8 best teams in third place overall also move on. Now we have 32 teams left, and things get spicy.

Step 2: The Knockout Rounds

Now it is one loss, and you are out. This is the part where fans bite their nails and coaches suddenly look ten years older.

- Round of 32
- Round of 16
- Quarterfinals
- Semifinals
- Third-place match
- Final

If a knockout game is tied after 90 minutes, the teams play extra time: two 15-minute halves. Still tied? It moves to penalty kicks. Each team takes 5 kicks. Most goals wins.

Still tied?! One kick each, until someone wins.

The final winner lifts the World Cup trophy, the biggest prize in soccer!

Meet Group H

Spain arrive as the reigning European champions and one of the most decorated footballing nations in history. Uruguay bring two World Cup titles and a reputation for punching above their weight. Saudi Arabia have already shown they can shock the world on the biggest stage. Cape Verde step into their first World Cup with nothing to lose and everything to prove.

Four teams. Three matches each. Two places in the knockout rounds.

On paper, Spain lead the way. But tournaments are not played on paper. Uruguay have built their identity on resilience. Saudi Arabia thrive when expectations are low. Cape Verde arrive as unknowns with belief and momentum.

By the end of matchday three, the table will decide everything. Until then, every team still has a path.

Spain

Spain do not come into this tournament rebuilding. They arrive as European champions after winning Euro 2024 in Berlin, and as one of the strongest sides in world football today.

La Roja have won the World Cup once, in 2010, and the European Championship four times in 1964, 2008, 2012, and 2024. Their golden era between 2008 and 2012 reshaped international football, and the current generation has brought them back to the top.

This is a team built on control, precision, and confidence in possession. They dictate games. They wear opponents down. And when they find rhythm, they are extremely difficult to stop.

In Group H, Spain are the reference point. Every other team will measure themselves against them.

Cabo Verde

Cape Verde arrive at their first ever World Cup as one of the smallest nations in the tournament. A country of just over half a million people, spread across islands in the Atlantic, now stepping onto football's biggest stage.

Their rise has been steady rather than sudden. They reached the quarter-finals of the Africa Cup of Nations on their debut in 2013 and again in 2023. Their squad is built largely from players developed across Europe, combined with a strong collective identity.

There is no long World Cup history here. No past campaigns to lean on. Just a team that has earned its place and is determined to compete.

Cape Verde are not expected to advance. That may be exactly what makes them dangerous.

Saudi Arabia

Saudi Arabia arrive at their seventh World Cup with growing belief. Their 2-1 victory over Argentina in 2022 remains one of the biggest upsets in tournament history and changed how the football world views them.

Their best World Cup performance came in 1994, when they reached the round of sixteen. Since then, results have varied, but the development of football in the country has accelerated, supported by investment and a more competitive domestic league.

Saudi Arabia are disciplined, organized, and capable of sudden impact. They do not need many chances. And when they find momentum, they can shift a game quickly.

In a group with Spain and Uruguay, their margin for error is small. But they have already shown they can rise to moments like this.

Uruguay

Uruguay carry one of the richest histories in world football. World champions in 1930 and 1950, they also claim Olympic gold medals in 1924 and 1928, achievements recognized as part of the early global game.

A nation of just over three million people, yet consistently competitive at the highest level. Uruguay's identity is clear. Tough to break down. Relentless in duels. Unfazed by reputation.

In modern tournaments, they have regularly reached the knockout stages, including a semi-final run in 2010 and multiple quarter-final appearances. Under Marcelo Bielsa, they bring intensity, structure, and clarity of purpose.

Uruguay do not adjust to opponents. They impose themselves. And they believe they can compete with anyone in this group.

Head-to-Head History

Group H brings a mix of established history and complete unknowns.

Cape Verde have never faced Spain, Saudi Arabia, or Uruguay. Every one of their matches in this group will be a first meeting.

Spain and Uruguay share the deepest history. Their meetings stretch back decades, including a 2-2 draw at the 1950 World Cup and a 0-0 draw in 1990. In more recent encounters, Spain have had the stronger record, including a 2-1 win at the 2013 Confederations Cup.

Spain and Saudi Arabia have met three times, with Spain winning all three, including a 1-0 victory at the 2006 World Cup.

Uruguay and Saudi Arabia met most notably at the 2018 World Cup, where Uruguay won 1-0 in the group stage. Their overall meetings are limited, but Uruguay hold the edge.

Three matchups come with history. Three will be played for the first time. In a group like this, both can matter.

Who's Played Who?

Some teams go way back. Others? Total strangers.
Here's how many times they've faced off.

	SPAIN	CABO VERDE	SAUDI ARABIA	URUGUAY
SPAIN		*Never met*	**3** 3W · 0D · 0L	**10** 5W · 5D · 0L
CABO VERDE	*Never met*		*Never met*	*Never met*
SAUDI ARABIA	**3** 0W · 0D · 3L	*Never met*		**3** 0W · 1D · 2L
URUGUAY	**10** 0W · 5D · 5L	*Never met*	**3** 2W · 1D · 0L	

Fun Fan Facts:
The Unofficial World Cup Edition

Spain

Everything Young Spain Fans Should Know

By: Jake Liam

THE WORLD CUP BY THE NUMBERS

MOST WORLD CUP WINS

Stars=Titles

★★★★★ BRAZIL

☆★★★★ GERMANY, ITALY

☆☆★★★ ARGENTINA

☆☆☆★★ FRANCE, URUGUAY

☆☆☆☆★ ENGLAND, SPAIN

GLOBAL REACH

5 BILLION
People Reached (2022)

1.5 BILLION
Watched the 2022 Final

1930 TO TODAY

1930 — 1st World Cup

1970 — Pele's 3rd Ttile

1982 — Expands to 24 Teams

2022 — Legendary Final

48 | 8 | 22

48 Teams Competing in 2026

8 Countries Ever to Win It

22 World Cups Played*

** No World Cup was played in 1942 and 1946 due to World War II.*
** 2026 will be the 23rd World Cup*

WINNER BY YEAR

1930 – Uruguay
1934 – Italy
1938 – Italy
1950 – Uruguay
1954 – West Germany
1958 – Brazil
1962 – Brazil
1966 – England
1970 – Brazil
1974 – West Germany

1978 – Argentina
1982 – Italy
1986 – Argentina
1990 – West Germany
1994 – Brazil
1998 – France
2002 – Brazil
2006 – Italy
2010 – Spain
2014 – Germany
2018 – France
2022 – Argentina

SPAIN
AT THE WORLD CUP

- FIRST PLAYED: 1934
- WINNER: 2010
- APPEARANCES: 16

7-0 Biggest Win Vs. Costa Rica (2022)

ALL-TIME MOST WORLD CUP GOALS

MIROSLAV KLOSE **(16)** ⚽ RONALDO NAZÁRIO **(15)** ⚽ GERD MÜLLER **(14)**

Spain Facts

Capital

Madrid

Population

about 47 million

National Sports

football (by far the most popular), basketball, tennis, cycling

Famous Food

paella, tapas, churros, jamón ibérico, tortilla española

Region / Conference

Europe / UEFA

Chapter 1: The Birth of La Roja

1. Spain's First Match in 1920: A Surprising Beginning

When Spain played its first official match in 1920, nobody was expecting a moment that would change the country's football future. The team was brand new, barely trained together, and had no reputation in international football. Most fans saw the tournament as a learning experience, not a place for surprises.

Then Spain played Denmark. And everything changed.

In their first-ever official match, Spain defeated one of Europe's strongest teams 1 - 0. The result shocked the football world. What was supposed to be a quiet debut instantly turned into a statement. Spain went on to win the silver medal at the Olympics, returning home as unexpected heroes.

Newspapers called them "The Heroes of Antwerp," after the city where the match was played, and fans across the country suddenly felt something click. Football was no longer just a game played in pockets of Spain. It was becoming a shared national passion. That single goal in Antwerp did more than win a match. It sparked belief, and Spain's long football journey had officially begun.

2. Why They're Called "La Roja"

Spain's nickname, "La Roja," means "The Red One," and it comes from their famous all-red kit. But early in their history, Spain's kit was not always red. In fact, there was a time when the team lined up in yellow, a strange chapter we'll come back to later... Over time, though, the red shirt became central to Spain's identity.

The color came to represent much more than a shirt. Spain is a country of different regions, languages, and traditions, but La Roja gave fans one team to rally around. When the national team played, the red jersey became a symbol of unity, pride, and shared belief across the country.

Today, when fans chant "¡Vamos, La Roja!" they are not just cheering for a team. They are calling on a shared identity built over generations. The color never changed again. And neither did what it came to mean.

they kicked off a century of football magic. These early players were the foundation of everything that came next, helping Spain begin a journey that would one day lead to world champions. *Photo: Spanish national football team in the 1920--21 season. Public domain. Source: Wikimedia Commons.*

3. Spain's Football Revolution of the 2000s

For years, Spain kept arriving at major tournaments with talent, hope, and the same painful ending. They played beautiful football, produced brilliant players, and were often labeled favorites. Then came the familiar moment when everything stopped. Another early exit. Another long trip home.

Fans started calling it the "quarter-final curse." No matter how strong the squad looked, Spain always seemed to fall at the same hurdle. The frustration grew louder with every tournament. People began to wonder if Spain would ever turn skill into success on the biggest stage.

Then, in the early 2000s, Spanish football made a bold decision. Instead of changing coaches every few years or chasing quick fixes, the country committed to a long-term plan.

Spain chose patience over panic.

Youth academies, coaches, and clubs across the country focused on technique, intelligence, and teamwork. Players were taught to stay calm under pressure, keep the ball moving, and trust each other completely. Winning mattered, but playing the right way mattered more.

That shift changed everything. Spain did not just become harder to beat. They became unmistakable. This revolution did not just help Spain win trophies. It gave them a way to play that finally felt like theirs.

4. The Rise of Tiki-Taka

"Tiki-taka" became the style that defined Spain's golden era. The name "tiki-taka" did not come from a coach's notebook. It came from the sound of the ball moving. Tiki. Taka. Pass after pass, never stopping. Spanish commentators started using the phrase during matches, and once fans heard it, the name stuck. It looks calm. It definitely isn't.

Tiki-taka was built on short passes, constant movement, and complete control of the ball. Instead of rushing forward or relying on strength, Spain focused on patience. Keep the ball. Move together. Wait for the right moment.

By the mid-2000s, this approach had fully taken shape, and by 2008 the name tiki-taka stuck. The roots of tiki-taka can be traced back to Dutch "total football," especially through Johan Cruyff's influence at FC Barcelona. But Spain made the style their own. Spanish teams emphasized intelligence, timing, and trust. Every pass had a purpose, and every player was part of the plan.

Watching Spain play tiki-taka often felt like watching a problem being solved in real time. Opponents chased, pressed, and guessed. Spain stayed calm. The ball moved faster than defenders ever could, and openings appeared when patience finally paid off.

Soon, tiki-taka was more than a tactic. It became Spain's identity. The style frustrated opponents, thrilled fans, and changed how football was played at every level. Spain did not just win by playing tiki-taka. They showed the world that control, intelligence, and belief could be just as powerful as speed or strength.

5. Spain's Youth Factory: Where Stars Are Built

The real engine behind Spain's success starts when players are still kids. Instead of long lectures or fitness tests, young players spend hours playing small-sided games where the ball is always moving and decisions have to be made fast. Touch the ball. Pass. Move. Think. Every second matters.

Coaches care less about how big or strong a player is and more about how calm and creative they are with the ball. Mistakes are part of learning, not something to fear. By the time these players grow up, staying cool under pressure feels natural.

Much of this system took shape in the 1990s and early 2000s, as Spain rebuilt its football identity from the ground up. This approach starts early. Young players are encouraged to keep the ball close, pass quickly, and understand space on the field. Mistakes are part of the process. Learning how to solve problems matters more than winning youth matches. Over time, this method produces players who are comfortable in tight spaces and confident in big moments.

La Masia, Barcelona's famous youth academy, produced legends like Xavi, Iniesta, and Busquets, but it is far from the only source of talent. Real Madrid, Athletic Club, Villarreal, Sevilla, and Valencia all developed players who shaped the national team. Spain's success was never about one club. It was about a shared philosophy across the country.

Because of this system, Spain rarely runs out of technically brilliant midfielders. Generations change, but the ideas stay the same. When new players arrive, they already understand how Spain wants to play. That consistency is not an accident. It is the foundation that turned belief into dominance.

Chapter 2: Legends of Spain

6. Iker Casillas: Spain's Quiet Guardian (2000-2016)

Iker Casillas grew up in the working-class neighborhood of Móstoles, just outside Madrid, dreaming of football like millions of Spanish kids. By the time he was a teenager, his dream was already moving fast. Casillas joined Real Madrid's youth academy and made his professional debut at just 18 years old. In 2000, he earned his first cap for Spain. A new era had quietly begun.

Casillas became Spain's goalkeeper during a time when pressure followed the team everywhere. Spain had talent, but big tournaments often ended in disappointment. As the years passed, Casillas grew into the role, becoming captain and emotional anchor. He was calm when matches were tight and fearless when everything was on the line.

His defining moments came on the biggest stages. At the 2008 European Championship, Casillas made a crucial save in the penalty shootout against Italy, helping Spain break through a long history of heartbreak. Two years later, in the 2010 World Cup final, he produced one of the most famous saves in football history, blocking Netherland's Arjen Robben in a one-on-one that could have changed everything. After moments like these, fans began calling him "Saint Iker." It wasn't a joke or a nickname he asked for. It was a thank-you, given to a goalkeeper who always seemed to be there when Spain needed him most. Spain went on to win 1 - 0 and lift their first World Cup.

Casillas played 167 matches for Spain, more than any other goalkeeper in the team's history. But numbers never told the full story. His presence gave teammates confidence. His saves protected belief. In a team built on patience and control, Iker Casillas was the calm that made greatness possible. And when pressure arrived, Spain trusted him completely.

7. Xavi Hernández: The Player Who Slowed the Game Down (2000-2014)

Xavi Hernández grew up in Terrassa, a town outside Barcelona, where football was less about power and more about thinking ahead. From a young age, coaches noticed something different. Xavi was not the fastest or strongest player on the field. But he always seemed to know where the ball should go next.

He came through FC Barcelona's famous youth academy, La Masia, where intelligence and technique mattered as much as talent. When Xavi reached the national team, Spain was still searching for an identity. Matches felt rushed. Big moments felt tense. Xavi brought calm into the middle of the chaos.

What made Xavi special was his control of time and space. He rarely lost the ball. He passed it quickly, moved into the right position, and kept Spain playing on their own terms. When Xavi was on the field, Spain did not panic. They passed. They waited. They trusted the plan. Spain stopped rushing. Opponents started chasing.

During Spain's golden era, Xavi became the heartbeat of the team. He controlled matches in the 2008 European Championship, the 2010 World Cup, and the 2012 Euros. Fans sometimes joked that watching Xavi was like watching a conductor lead an orchestra. He did not need to score goals to decide games. He decided how the game felt.

Xavi played more than 130 matches for Spain, but his true impact cannot be measured by numbers. He gave Spain control. He gave them patience. And once Spain learned how to control games, they learned how to win them.

8. Andrés Iniesta: The Artist (2006-2018)

The clock was ticking. Legs were tired. The stadium was loud enough to shake your chest. When Spain needed someone who would not rush, panic, or hide, Andrés Iniesta stepped forward.

Iniesta came from the small town of Fuentealbilla, far from big stadiums and bright lights. As a kid, he was quiet, shy, and smaller than many of the players around him. He did not look like a superstar. He did not play like one either. He played smarter.

He rose through FC Barcelona's youth system and joined the national team during Spain's transformation years. Iniesta never forced the game. He slipped into space, kept the ball moving, and made hard moments feel simple. When pressure built, he stayed calm. Always.

Iniesta scored the most important goal in Spain's history. In the 2010 World Cup final, with just minutes left in extra time, the ball fell to him inside the box. He did not rush. He did not smash it. He placed it perfectly into the net. Spain had its first-ever world championship.

The celebration exploded across the country. Streets filled. People cried. And then Iniesta did something unforgettable. He lifted his jersey to reveal a shirt honoring his close friend Dani Jarque, who had passed away the year before. In the loudest moment Spain had ever known, Iniesta chose quiet respect.

For Spanish fans, Andrés Iniesta will always be more than a footballer. He did not charge across the pitch. He seemed to float across it, finding space where others saw chaos. In the biggest moment of all, the gentle artist painted Spain's greatest sporting memory.

9. Sergio Busquets: The Player You Only Notice When He's Gone (2009-2020)

If Spain's midfield was a machine, Sergio Busquets was the quiet gear that kept it running. He did not score famous goals or steal headlines. Most of the time, he barely seemed to move. But without him, nothing worked.

Busquets grew up in Sabadell, near Barcelona, and came through FC Barcelona's youth system just like Xavi and Iniesta. When he joined the national team, Spain already had stars. What they needed was balance. Busquets played deeper than the others, reading danger before it appeared and stopping problems before they started.

He won the ball. He passed it safely. He chose the simple option again and again. That might not sound exciting, but it was powerful. With Busquets holding the middle, Xavi and Iniesta could control games without fear. Spain stayed calm because Busquets made calm possible.

During Spain's golden era, Busquets became the silent shield in front of the defense. Opponents tried to press. Spain played through them. Opponents tried to counter. Busquets was already there. He made difficult matches feel manageable and chaotic moments feel slow.

Busquets played more than 140 matches for Spain, but his true value showed up in the spaces between passes. When he was on the field, Spain looked balanced. When he was not, everyone noticed. That is the mark of a player who mastered the unseen side of greatness.

10. David Villa: Spain's Relentless Finisher (2005-2014)

David Villa is Spain's all-time leading goal scorer and one of the most dangerous forwards of his generation. When Spain needed goals, Villa delivered them. Calm finishes. Quick strikes. Big moments, again and again.

Fans nicknamed him "El Guaje," which means "The Kid," because he grew up playing football on the narrow streets of Asturias. The spaces were tight, the ground uneven, and mistakes were punished instantly. Those street games shaped how he played. Villa learned to shoot quickly, find space where none seemed to exist, and score from impossible angles. Curled shots. Volleys. Chips. Long-range strikes. He had every weapon.

During the 2010 World Cup, Villa carried Spain's attack with five vital goals. His finishing kept Spain alive through tense knockout matches and pushed them all the way to the final. Two years earlier at Euro 2008, Villa won the Golden Boot as the tournament's top scorer, announcing himself as the striker Spain had been waiting for.

Even though Spain has produced many brilliant forwards, no one matched Villa's combination of consistency, confidence, and big-game performances. He was the perfect striker for tiki-taka. While others controlled the game, David Villa finished it. And when Spain lifted its greatest trophies, his goals were already written all over them.

Chapter 3: Legendary Moments

11. Winning Euro 2008: The Curse Finally Breaks

By the time Euro 2008 arrived, Spain had spent decades wondering when belief would finally turn into a trophy. Fans called it the curse because Spain always seemed to lose in heartbreaking fashion. But in 2008 everything changed. Led by players like Casillas, Xavi, Iniesta, and Villa, Spain powered through the European Championship with confidence and style.

The final was against Germany who were considered stronger and more experienced. But Spain did not care. Something in the squad had changed. They controlled the game. With David Villa injured, Fernando Torres stepped in and scored the winning goal. When the final whistle blew, Spain had won their first major trophy in 44 years. Euro 2008 was not just a victory. It was the moment Spain stopped hoping and started expecting.

12. Spain's Narrow Path to the 2010 World Cup Final

Spain's World Cup nearly unraveled before it even began. A shock 1-0 loss to Switzerland in the opening match sent doubts racing through the squad and across the country. After years of waiting for a breakthrough, the familiar fear returned. Bars went quiet. Living rooms froze. Was this another tournament slipping away before it had truly started?

From that moment on, Spain responded the only way they knew how. They slowed the game down, trusted the ball, and refused to chase results. Every match became a test of patience and nerve. One goal had to be enough. One mistake could end everything.

As the tournament moved into the knockout rounds, the tension only grew. Spain edged past opponent after opponent, holding firm under pressure and staying true to their style. The margins were razor-thin. The control had to be perfect every single time.

There was no room to relax.

By the end of the run, Spain had survived every scare and answered every doubt. They reached the World Cup final where they would meet the Netherlands. Not by overpowering opponents, but by outlasting them. One more match stood between belief and history.

13. The 2010 World Cup Final: 116 Minutes of Waiting

The World Cup final did not feel fast. It felt heavy. Spain and the Netherlands battled through fouls, pressure, and nerves as the clock kept moving forward. Every pass mattered. Every mistake felt dangerous. Ninety minutes came and went with no goal, only tension. By that point, nobody was sitting anymore.

Extra time arrived, and the waiting grew louder. Players were exhausted. Legs burned. Fans barely breathed. Spain stayed patient, moving the ball, trusting the plan they had spent years building. The moment had not arrived yet. But it was coming.

In the 116th minute, it finally did. One opening. One chance. One strike. Spain had waited a lifetime for this moment, and they did not miss it. When the ball hit the net, everything released at once. Joy. Relief. History.

The final whistle followed soon after. Spain were world champions for the first time. Not because they rushed. Not because they panicked. But because they believed in their way of playing until the very end.

For Spanish fans, those 116 minutes are unforgettable. They were not just watching a match. They were watching patience turn into a world title.

14. Euro 2012: When Spain Became Untouchable

By the time Euro 2012 arrived, Spain were no longer chasing belief. They were defending it. Everyone knew how they played. Everyone knew what was coming. And still, no one could stop it.

Spain controlled matches with a calm that felt almost unfair. They passed, waited, and moved opponents out of position again and again. Pressure did not shake them. Big stages did not rush them. The game bent to Spain's rhythm, not the other way around.

The final against Italy made it impossible to argue. Spain dominated from start to finish, winning 4-0 in one of the most complete performances ever seen in a major tournament final. It was not just a win. It was a statement. Spain was not surviving anymore. They were fully in control.

Euro 2012 confirmed what fans had started to believe years earlier. This was not a lucky run or a perfect moment. This was a team at the peak of its powers, playing football on its own terms. Spain were champions again, and this time, it felt inevitable.

15. The Shock of 2014: When the Champions Fell

After dominating international football for six straight years, Spain arrived at the 2014 World Cup as one of the favorites. Fans believed the magic could continue. But football has a way of reminding everyone that nothing lasts forever.

Spain's opening match against the Netherlands was shocking. A 5-1 loss stunned fans around the world and felt like a turning point. The team that once controlled every moment suddenly looked a step behind. The calm was gone. The rhythm was off. Something had changed.

A second loss to Chile sent Spain out of the tournament in the group stage, an outcome that once seemed unthinkable. It was a difficult ending to one of the greatest eras the sport had ever seen. But it was also a reminder of how quickly football moves forward.

The 2014 World Cup did not erase what Spain had achieved. It simply marked the end of a chapter. New players would rise. New ideas would form. The golden era had closed, but the story was far from over.

16. The Anthem with No Words

Spain has one of the few national anthems in the world with no official lyrics. It is called the Marcha Real, and fans have debated for decades about whether it should ever have words at all. Several attempts have been made to add lyrics, but none were accepted by the public. Some versions were too political, others too emotional, and some just did not feel like Spain.

And yet, when it plays, everybody listens. During matches, fans often hum or chant along to the melody which creates a unique atmosphere. When La Roja lines up before a big game, the stadium fills with a powerful roar that needs no words. The anthem without lyrics has become part of the team's identity. It is simple, proud, and instantly recognizable.

17. Spain Has No Official Home Stadium

Unlike many national teams, Spain does not have one permanent home stadium. Instead, La Roja plays matches in cities across the country including Madrid, Seville, Valencia, Bilbao, Barcelona, and La Coruña. This tradition began in part to make sure fans from every region could experience the national team live.

One stadium that developed a special reputation is the Ramón Sánchez Pizjuán in Seville. Spain's record there is incredibly strong and many fans believe the atmosphere gives the team extra confidence. Some places just feel lucky. Rotating stadiums has helped Spain stay connected to the entire country. Wherever they play, the stands are filled with red shirts and loud support.

18. Superstitions Inside the Spain Camp

Football players can be extremely superstitious and Spain's players are no different. Over the years, some players have had lucky socks, wristbands, or even the same pre-match meals. Iker Casillas was known for touching the crossbar before kickoff. Andrés Iniesta wore the same pair of boots for several games in a row during the 2010 World Cup because he believed they brought him good fortune.

During major tournaments, players often sit in the same seats on the team bus or follow the same warmup routines. Some superstitions might sound unusual, but the players believe in them. When footballers feel lucky, they rarely question it. These rituals add a fun and human side to Spain's otherwise calm and controlled playing style.

19. The Power of the Academies

Spain's success is deeply connected to its football academies. La Masia in Barcelona and Real Madrid's academy are the most famous, but clubs across the country have also played huge roles in developing talent. Villarreal, Sevilla, Athletic Club, Real Sociedad and Valencia all produce players who regularly reach the national team.

Spain's golden generation was built from these academies. Xavi and Iniesta came from La Masia. Iker Casillas came from Real Madrid. David Silva came from Valencia's academy. Sergio Busquets and Jordi Alba developed in Barcelona's youth system. The national team feels like a partnership between rival clubs where everyone contributes to the greater good. Rivalries disappeared when the national shirt came on. When Spain succeeds, the entire football system behind it celebrates.

20. The Red Shirt and the Time Spain Wore Yellow

Spain's red jersey is one of the most iconic kits in world football. But it wasn't always that way.

Today, fans instantly recognize the bright red top and dark blue shorts that La Roja usually wears. But there was a period in the 1950s when Spain wore yellow instead of red. The switch to yellow happened for a practical reason. Red sometimes clashed with other teams on early black-and-white television broadcasts, and yellow was easier to see.

On screens it made sense. In the stands, it felt strange. Fans were used to red. Seeing Spain run out in yellow caught people off guard, and the color never truly felt like home. The experiment did not last long. Before long, Spain returned to the red shirt supporters recognized and loved.

That return mattered. Red became more than a uniform. It became a symbol. Every major trophy of Spain's golden era was won wearing red, and over time the color came to represent unity, passion, and national pride. When Spain lines up in red today, it feels permanent, like the team has finally found the color it was always meant to wear.

Chapter 5: Today and Tomorrow

21. The Rise of Pedri and Gavi

Spain's new generation began attracting attention when two teenage midfielders, Pedri and Gavi, stepped into the spotlight. Both players came through Barcelona's academy and were praised for their calmness and technique even at such young ages. And neither looked overwhelmed for a second. Pedri became known for his smooth passing and mature decision making while Gavi impressed everyone with his energy, bravery and relentless pressure on the ball.

Fans and coaches quickly noticed how similar they were to the legendary midfielders of Spain's golden era. Many compared Pedri to Iniesta and Gavi to a young Xavi because of the way they controlled play. These comparisons brought pressure, but the two teenagers embraced it with confidence. Together, they reminded Spain that the future of the midfield was in good hands.

22. Luis Enrique's Modern Makeover

When Luis Enrique took over as Spain's head coach in 2018, he faced a tricky challenge. Spain still believed in possession and control, but the game around them had changed. Opponents were faster, more aggressive, and less patient. Spain needed to evolve without losing who they were.

Luis Enrique kept the heart of Spain's style but pushed it forward. He asked players to move the ball quicker, press higher, and attack with more speed. Young players were trusted early, sometimes earlier than anyone expected. The message was clear. Play bravely. Take responsibility. Do not wait for permission.

The results were not always perfect, but the direction was clear. Spain played with energy again. They pressed together, defended as a unit, and showed confidence against top opponents. At Euro 2020, the team reached the semifinals and pushed eventual champions Italy all the way to penalties.

Spain did not lift the trophy, but something important returned. Belief. Under Luis Enrique, Spain looked brave again. The rebuild was no longer just a plan. It was happening on the field.

23. The 2018 World Cup Coaching Chaos

Just days before the 2018 World Cup began, Spain shocked the football world by firing their head coach Julen Lopetegui. Lopetegui had already agreed to take over at Real Madrid after the tournament. When the Spanish Football Federation learned of the decision, they chose to remove him immediately.

The timing could not have been more difficult. Players had prepared for months under one coach, and suddenly everything changed. Fernando Hierro stepped in with almost no time to adjust tactics or calm nerves.

The focus shifted from football to uncertainty. Spain still showed moments of quality during the tournament, moving the ball well and controlling long stretches of play. But the sudden change made it hard to build rhythm or confidence. Their World Cup ended in a penalty shootout loss to host nation Russia in the round of sixteen.

The experience became an important lesson. Talent alone is not enough at the highest level. Stability, trust, and unity off the field matter just as much as what happens on it. For Spain, 2018 was a reminder that preparation and calm are part of winning too.

24. Euro 2020 and the Return of Belief

Euro 2020 was a turning point for the new era of Spain. The team was young, hungry and eager to prove they belonged among Europe's best. Spain started the tournament slowly but grew stronger with every match. Players like Pedri, Dani Olmo and Ferran Torres showed maturity beyond their years. The team reached the semifinals where they faced Italy in a tense match that went all the way to penalties.

Even though Spain lost the shootout, the tournament restored belief across the country. Fans saw a team full of potential and character. Spain no longer looked like a nation living in the shadow of its golden generation. Euro 2020 showed that the rebuild was working and that the future was bright. The climb had started.

25. The Road to World Cup 2026: Could Spain Go All the Way?

As Spain looks toward the 2026 World Cup, the feeling around the team is different than it was a decade earlier. There is less pressure to repeat the past and more excitement about what could come next. A new generation has already stepped onto the world stage, and they are learning fast.

Young stars like Pedri and Gavi have shown they belong at the highest level, while players such as Lamine Yamal, Nico Williams, and Alejandro Balde bring speed, creativity, and fearlessness. Many of them grew up watching Spain's golden era and now carry its ideas into a new version of the team.

Spain's style continues to evolve. Possession still matters, but the team now plays with more pace and direct movement. The youth system remains strong, and competition for places is fierce. Nothing is guaranteed, but the pieces are coming together.

Spain may not arrive at 2026 shouting about favorites or making bold predictions on social media, but they will arrive prepared. This is a team that understands how quickly football turns and how carefully success must be rebuilt. What remains constant is belief, patience, and a system designed to keep producing elite players.

The next chapter is still unwritten, but Spain knows how to write it. They've been here before. And when the tournament begins, the real question won't be whether Spain can compete. It will be whether anyone can stop them when it matters most

Bonus Trivia Quiz!

You think you are a true Spain fan? Try this bonus quiz!

1. When did Spain play their first official international match?

A) 1912
B) 1920
C) 1930
D) 1909

2. What is the nickname of the Spain national team?

A) La Dorada
B) La Roja
C) Los Toros
D) La Furia Blanca

3. Who scored the winning goal in the 2010 World Cup Final?

A) Fernando Torres
B) Andrés Iniesta
C) David Villa
D) Pedro

4. Which goalkeeper is known as "San Iker"?

A) David de Gea

B) Pepe Reina

C) Iker Casillas

D) Unai Simón

5. Spain won Euro 2008 by defeating which country in the final?

A) Italy

B) Germany

C) France

D) Portugal

6. What style of play became the trademark of Spain's golden era?

A) Catenaccio

B) Tiki taka

C) Route One

D) Gegenpressing

7. Which two young stars are seen as the heirs to Spain's midfield legacy?

A) Rodri and Koke

B) Pedri and Gavi

C) Llorente and Olmo

D) Silva and Mata

8. Who is Spain's all time leading goal scorer?

A) Raúl

B) David Villa

C) Fernando Torres

D) Álvaro Morata

9. Spain's 2012 Euro Final victory ended with what score?

A) 3--1

B) 1--0

C) 4--0

D) 2--2

10. Which nation ended Spain's long unbeaten run in 2009?

A) Brazil

B) United States

C) Germany

D) Netherlands

11. Who was Spain's captain during their 2010 World Cup triumph?

A) Xavi

B) Sergio Ramos

C) Iker Casillas

D) Carles Puyol

12. What unusual fact is true about Spain's national anthem?

A) It is the shortest anthem in Europe
B) It was written by Picasso
C) It has no official lyrics
D) It is only played at home games

13. Which manager led Spain through their Euro 2020 revival?

A) Vicente del Bosque
B) Luis Enrique
C) Julen Lopetegui
D) Fernando Hierro

14. In what round was Spain eliminated during the 2018 World Cup?

A) Group Stage
B) Round of Sixteen
C) Quarterfinals
D) Semifinals

15. Which Spain forward won the Golden Boot at Euro 2008?

A) Fernando Torres
B) Álvaro Morata
C) David Villa
D) Dani Olmo

Super Fan Secret Challenge

Only a true Spain fan will know this.

(No Answer Provided)

- 53 -

What year was La Masia's modern academy building officially opened?

A) 1979
B) 1984
C) 1991
D) 1998

Answer Key

1. B) 1920

2. B) La Roja

3. B) Andrés Iniesta

4. C) Iker Casillas

5. B) Germany

6. B) Tiki taka

7. B) Pedri and Gavi

8. B) David Villa

9. C) 4--0

10. B) United States

11. C) Iker Casillas

12. C) It has no official lyrics

13. B) Luis Enrique

14. B) Round of Sixteen

15. C) David Villa

Fun Fan Facts:
The Unofficial World Cup Edition

Cape Verde

Everything Young Cape Verde Fans Should Know

By: Jake Liam

THE WORLD CUP
BY THE NUMBERS

MOST WORLD CUP WINS
Stars=Titles

★★★★★ BRAZIL
☆★★★★ GERMANY, ITALY
☆☆★★★ ARGENTINA
☆☆☆★★ FRANCE, URUGUAY
☆☆☆☆★ ENGLAND, SPAIN

GLOBAL REACH

5 BILLION
People Reached
(2022)

1.5 BILLION
Watched the
2022 Final

1930 TO TODAY

1930
1st World
Cup

1970
Pele's 3rd
Ttile

1982
Expands to
24 Teams

2022
Legendary
Final

48 | 8 | 22

Teams Competing in 2026 | **Countries Ever to Win It** | **World Cups Played***

* No World Cup was played in 1942 and 1946 due to World War II.
* 2026 will be the 23rd World Cup

WINNER BY YEAR

1930 – Uruguay
1934 – Italy
1938 – Italy
1950 – Uruguay
1954 – West Germany
1958 – Brazil
1962 – Brazil
1966 – England
1970 – Brazil
1974 – West Germany

1978 – Argentina
1982 – Italy
1986 – Argentina
1990 – West Germany
1994 – Brazil
1998 – France
2002 – Brazil
2006 – Italy
2010 – Spain
2014 – Germany
2018 – France
2022 – Argentina

CAPE VERDE
AT THE WORLD CUP

- FIRST PLAYED: 2026
- BEST FINISH: NEVER PARTICIPATED
- APPEARANCES: 0

0
Goals conceded
during the 2026
qualifying run

ALL-TIME MOST WORLD CUP GOALS

MIROSLAV KLOSE **(16)** ⚽ RONALDO NAZÁRIO **(15)** ⚽ GERD MÜLLER **(14)**

Cape Verde Facts

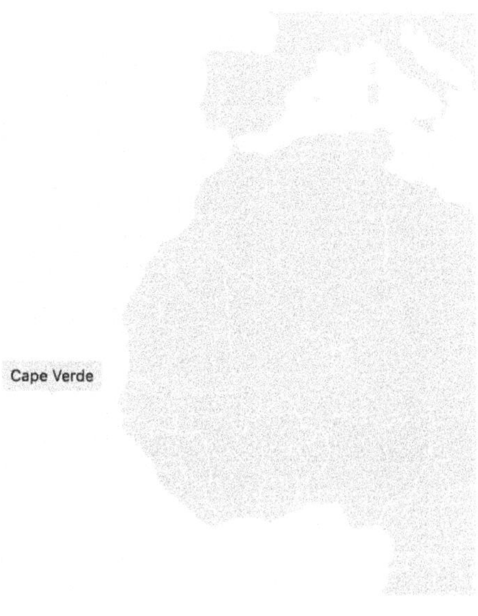

Capital

Praia

Population

about 500,000

National Sports

football

Famous Foods

cachupa, pastel com diablo dentro, grilled seafood

Region / Conference

Africa / CAF

Chapter 1: Born Between Islands and Oceans

1. When Football Found the Islands

Football did not arrive in Cape Verde with fireworks and a ribbon cutting. It showed up like a new kid on the block with a ball under its arm. Ports, schools, dusty corners, anywhere people had a little space and a lot of curiosity. And once it started rolling, it did not stop.

The best part is how little football needs. You do not need a fancy field. You need a ball. You need friends. You need that one kid who always says, "Next goal wins." In Cape Verde, the game fit island life perfectly because it can happen anywhere, anytime, with whatever you have.

So football did not just get played. It got adopted. Like, "Congrats. You live here now."

2. Small Islands Make Fast Brains and Quick Feet

Cape Verde is an island nation made up of ten islands, each with its own vibe. So it's not endless wide-open land. That means space can be tight. And when space is tight, football gets spicy fast. You cannot take ten touches to decide what you want to do. Someone will steal it on touch number three and then grin at you forever.

Players learn a different superpower. Control. Quick decisions. A first touch that does not bounce away like a startled rabbit. When you grow up playing in small spaces, you get good at tiny moves that make a big difference.

It is like learning to dance in a crowded room. You figure it out. You get smooth. And suddenly you are the one everyone is watching.

3. Independence Made the Shirt Real

Cape Verde became independent from Portugal in 1975. That is the moment the national team shirt starts to mean something huge. Before independence, there was no Cape Verde national team to represent the islands as a country. No anthem before kickoff. No flag on the chest. Talented players existed, but the team identity was not official yet.

After its independence, the idea of "We are Cape Verde" could finally step onto a pitch. That changes how people feel about football. It is not only a game anymore. It is pride. It is belonging. It is every island connected by one badge.

A national team is basically a moving flag. Cape Verde finally got to raise it.

4. From Sand to Hard Ground, the Ball Does Whatever It Wants

In Cape Verde, the pitch does not always look like a perfect green carpet. Sometimes it is sand, which turns sprinting into a workout you did not ask for. Sometimes it is hard ground, where the ball can bounce like it just drank three sodas.

That training, Miyagi-style. Sand builds balance. Hard ground builds control. Weird bounces teach you to stay calm when the game gets chaotic. You learn to adjust, not complain. You learn to solve the problem.

Then you step onto a smooth stadium field later and think, "Oh wow. This is the luxury version."

5. Why They're Called the Blue Sharks

Cape Verde's nickname is the Blue Sharks, and that is not a "cute mascot" kind of name. Sharks are always moving. Always alert. Always ready. They do not need to be the biggest thing in the ocean to be dangerous. They just need the right moment.

That fits Cape Verde. A smaller nation on the world map, but not small in spirit. When they smell a chance, they go for it. Fast. Fearless. No hesitation. It is island football with teeth.

6. Pedro Brito: The Captain Who Came Back to Build (1989-2005)

Pedro Leitão Brito, known to everyone as Bubista, grew up on the island of Boa Vista and became a central defender, the player responsible for stopping danger before it turns into panic.

When he played for Cape Verde, the national team was still figuring itself out. Bubista led by being calm when matches got loud and serious when moments mattered most.

After his playing career ended, he did something rare. He came back as a coach. Same badge, same responsibility, just from the sideline. That is not just leadership. That is commitment.

7. Elvis Macedo: The Midfield Engine That Never Quit (2007-2019)

Elvis Manuel Monteiro Macedo, better known as Babanco, was born in Praia and made midfield his home. Midfield is football's busiest job. You defend, you attack, and you connect everything in between.

Babanco was never about flashy moments. He was about keeping the team steady. When the game got frantic, he slowed it down and made things make sense again.

And yes, with a name like Elvis, you can say this much. He did not leave the building early. He stayed until the job was done.

8. Fernando Varela: The Wall Who Chose the Badge (2008-2019)

Fernando Varela, often called Stopira, was born in Portugal but chose to represent Cape Verde. That decision reflects what this team is built on. Islands, family roots, and identity that travels.

As a center-back, he organized the defense, talked constantly, and made sure mistakes did not pile up. When pressure rose, he brought control.

Defenders do not get many cheers. Their highlights are quiet ones. A blocked shot. A cleared cross. An attacker shaking their head and turning away.

- 66 -

9. Josimar Dias: The Calm Behind the Chaos (2012--)

Josimar José Évora Dias, known as Vozinha, became one of Cape Verde's most important goalkeepers. Goalkeepers live in a different world. They stand alone and stay calm while chaos runs straight at them.

When Vozinha became the regular presence at the back, the team changed. Defenders trusted him. The whole group played braver.

A big save does more than stop a goal. It sends a message. "We can survive this." Vozinha sent that message often.

10. Ryan Mendes: Records, Speed, and Island Freedom (2010--)

Ryan Mendes was born in Mindelo, a port city on the island of São Vicente, where music, movement, and football spill into everyday life. He came through Batuque FC before taking his game far beyond the islands.

He plays as a winger, which means speed, direct runs, and fearlessness. The kind of player who makes defenders backpedal like they just remembered they left the stove on.

Over time, Mendes became Cape Verde's most-capped player and all-time top scorer. A cap simply means an appearance for the national team, and earning the most means he was trusted year after year.

He also built a long professional career in Europe, playing in countries like France and Turkey, showing his style worked against top-level competition.

Records sound serious. Mendes plays like a kid who remembers goals made of shoes. Run at you. Try something bold. Smile when it works. That joy is part of what makes Cape Verde dangerous.

Chapter 3: Moments That Made the World Look Twice

11. 2013: The First AFCON Ticket and a Group Nobody Expected

When Cape Verde qualified for the 2013 Africa Cup of Nations, it already felt historic. First appearance ever. New badge on a very big stage. But then the draw came out, and suddenly things felt very real. They were placed in a group with South Africa, the host nation, plus Morocco and Angola. No freebies. No easing in.

Then the games started. Cape Verde beat Angola 2 - 1 in their opening match. Not survived. Beat. They followed it with a 1 - 1 draw against Morocco, a team with deep AFCON history. After a loss to South Africa, the math came out clean. Cape Verde finished second in the group and moved on.

Three matches. One win. One draw. One loss. Enough to advance. Enough to announce themselves.

12. Quarterfinals on the First Try

Advancing from the group already turned heads. Reaching the quarterfinals in your very first AFCON appearance made people sit up straight.

Cape Verde's run ended against Ghana, one of Africa's traditional heavyweights.

Ghana brought experience and pace, and they made it count. Midway through the match, pressure finally broke through when Wakaso Mubarak stepped up and buried a penalty, forcing Cape Verde to chase the game. Instead of fading, Cape Verde pushed forward, testing Ghana's back line and trying to find a way back in. The match stayed tense until late, when Asamoah Gyan struck again, using his strength and timing to finish the move and seal it. Cape Verde kept fighting until the final whistle, tackling, pressing, and refusing to go quietly.

Ghana won 2 - 0. That was the end of the road. Even in defeat, the message stuck. Cape Verde had not been overrun. They had not looked lost. They had competed.

Very few debut teams reach the knockout stage, and even fewer do it without looking overwhelmed. Cape

Verde did both. They left South Africa as something new. A team opponents could respect.

13. Real Wins Against Real Teams

After AFCON 2013, Cape Verde stopped being a surprise and started becoming a problem. They beat Tunisia in competitive matches. They took points off Ghana. These were not friendlies where everyone experiments. These were games that counted.

The results added up fast. In February 2014, Cape Verde climbed to 27th in the FIFA world rankings, the highest in their history. That placed them above many nations with far larger populations and budgets.

Rankings are not vibes. They are math. And the math said Cape Verde was doing something right.

14. The Misses That Hurt the Most

Not every story climbs smoothly. Cape Verde came painfully close to the 2014 World Cup. On the field, they finished top of their qualifying group. Celebration followed. Then everything stopped.

Cape Verde were docked points for fielding an ineligible player earlier in qualifying. Just like that, they were out. No playoff. No second chance. One administrative mistake erased months of work. That one stung.

Then came AFCON 2015. Cape Verde lost all three group matches. But look closer. Tunisia beat them 2 - 1. Zambia beat them 1 - 0. DR Congo beat them 4 - 2. Competitive games. Small margins. Big lessons.

Sometimes growth hurts. This was one of those stretches.

15. From Surprise to Studied Opponent

The biggest change is not a trophy. It is preparation. Opponents no longer show up loose against Cape Verde. They watch film. They plan. They adjust.

That is respect. And respect is earned slowly, match by match.

Cape Verde's rise is built on real results. Group wins. Quarterfinals. Ranking jumps. Near misses that still mattered. This is not a fairy tale. It is a football build. And it is still going.

Cape Verde after a goal, and the celebration hits like a wave. Bodies flying into a group hug. Arms up. Faces screaming, "Yes, that just happened." This is not a quiet little fist pump. This is the Blue Sharks turning one moment into a whole-party memory. **Photo/** *Credit: Ethiopia vs Cape Verde, 9 January 2022. Cape Verde players celebrating a goal ("Jubilation de but"). Photo by Happiraphael (HappiRaphael Mbiele). © Wikimedia Commons.*

Chapter 4: Crests, Colors, Music, and the Fans

16. Ten Islands, One Nation

Cape Verde is not one place. It is ten main islands scattered across the Atlantic, separated by water, weather, and long stretches of sky. Getting from one island to another has always taken effort. Boats. Flights. Waiting. Planning. Distance is part of daily life.

That distance shapes the culture. Families often live on different islands. Friends grow up used to saying goodbye and meaning "see you later." People learn early that connection does not always mean closeness. It means commitment. You stay linked even when the ocean sits between you.

Football became one of the strongest ways to close those gaps. When the national team plays, it does not belong to one city or one island. It belongs to everyone at once. São Vicente. Santiago. Sal. Fogo. All watching the same match, reacting to the same moments, arguing about the same call.

For ninety minutes, the water disappears. The islands move together. That is why the national team matters so much in Cape Verde. It is one of the few times the entire country feels like it is standing in the same place.

17. The Flag and Crest, Explained Without Guessing

Cape Verde's flag is easy to picture once it is actually explained. The background is deep blue, like the Atlantic Ocean that surrounds the islands. Near the bottom runs a thin red stripe, bordered by two white stripes. Off to the left sits a circle of ten yellow stars. No animals. No shields. Just clean shapes that mean something.

The blue stands for the ocean and sky that connect the islands. The white stripes represent peace. The red stripe stands for effort and struggle, the work it takes to keep moving forward. The ten yellow stars each represent one of Cape Verde's islands, separate but arranged in a circle to show unity. Different places. Same country.

The football crest carries this same idea onto the shirt. When players wear it, they are not representing one city or one island. They are wearing the whole nation, simplified into colors and stars. Once you see it that way, the badge makes sense. And once it makes sense, it sticks.

18. The Sound of Football on the Islands

Football in Cape Verde does not happen in silence. It has a soundtrack. Drums. Clapping. Voices that rise and fall together. Even before kickoff, you can usually hear something nearby keeping time.

Music is part of everyday life on the islands, and it carries straight into the game. Styles like funaná, morna, and coladeira shape the rhythm people move to. Hand drums and percussion lead the sound, sometimes joined by whistles or chants that repeat and build. It is not organized like a choir. It is looser. Warmer. Alive.

That rhythm shows up on the field too. Cape Verdean players often look comfortable waiting on the ball, shifting their weight, changing pace suddenly. The game breathes. It speeds up. It slows down. There is patience mixed with surprise, the same way the music works.

For fans, the sound makes matches feel familiar. It feels like home. Football does not interrupt culture in Cape Verde. It joins it. Same rhythm. Same energy. Just a different stage.

19. Food, Noise, and Matchday Life

On matchday in Cape Verde, football does not happen on an empty stomach. Food and the game arrive together. Someone is always cooking. Something is always sizzling.

You might smell grilled fish near the coast or a pot of cachupa slowly working in the background. Cachupa, the country's national dish, is a slow-cooked stew made from corn, beans, and whatever meat, fish, or vegetables are on hand, the kind of food that simmers for hours and feeds everyone nearby.

People eat before kickoff, during halftime, and sometimes while yelling at the screen. Plates are shared. Drinks are passed. Nobody treats the match like a quiet appointment. It is a gathering.

Radios play when screens are not available. Televisions draw crowds when they are. Conversations overlap the commentary. Someone argues about a missed pass. Someone else laughs and waves it off. The game keeps going either way.

At the Estádio Nacional in Praia, the crowd feels close and personal. About fifteen thousand fans pack in tight, bringing drums, flags, food, and noise that turn the match into a full-body experience.

Football in Cape Verde fits into daily life the same way food does. It is not formal. It is not precious. It is meant to be shared. When the national team plays, the match feels less like an event and more like a long table where everyone has pulled up a chair.

20. An Island Nation That Shows Up Everywhere

Cape Verde's football family does not live in one place. Islanders have always traveled for work, opportunity, and connection, and they carried their football pride with them.

That means Cape Verde supporters show up far from home. In Portugal. In the Netherlands. In the United States. In France. Wherever the team plays, blue shirts appear. Flags get draped over shoulders. Someone starts a chant, even if they are outnumbered.

For players, that support matters. Away matches do not feel fully away. You hear familiar voices. You see familiar colors. The distance shrinks again.

The national team becomes a moving reunion. Different accents. Different cities. Same flag. Same songs. Same belief. Cape Verde might be made of islands, but when football is involved, the country travels as one.

Chapter 5: Today, Tomorrow, and What Comes Next

21. The Modern Blue Sharks Know Who They Are

Today's Cape Verde team does not feel like it is still asking for permission. They play with structure, confidence, and patience. Defensively organized. Comfortable on the ball. Ready to counter fast when space opens up.

This version of the Blue Sharks understands game management. When to slow things down. When to press. When to wait. That awareness comes from years of playing meaningful matches instead of just dreaming about them.

They are not chasing an identity anymore. They are playing inside one.

22. AFCON Is No Longer a Surprise Invite

Africa Cup of Nations qualification is no longer a shock headline for Cape Verde. It is an expectation. Recent campaigns have included wins against established teams and long stretches where the Blue Sharks controlled matches instead of reacting to them.

Cape Verde now enters qualifying groups knowing they can advance. That mindset shift is huge. Once belief becomes normal, performance usually follows.

Opponents feel it too. No more overlooking. No more easing in.

23. Young Players Arrive Already Believing

The next generation is growing up watching Cape Verde compete, not just participate. That changes everything. Young players now see national heroes who look like them, play like them, and came from places they recognize.

They arrive with confidence instead of nerves. They expect to belong. That belief shortens the gap between potential and performance. This is how football cultures level up quietly.

24. World Cup Dreams That Are No Longer Wild

Cape Verde has already tasted how close World Cup qualification can be. One mistake. One decision. One point. That memory stays sharp.

Now the conversation has changed. It is no longer "Could it ever happen?" It is "What needs to go right?" That is a very different place to stand.

The margins are still thin. The dream is still hard. But it is no longer distant.

25. Why Cape Verde's Story Still Feels Just Beginning

Cape Verde's football story is not about shortcuts or miracles. It is about building. Step by step. Tournament by tournament. Generation by generation.

Small islands. Big heart. Real results. A team that learned how to earn respect and then keep it.

The Blue Sharks are not finished. They are still swimming forward.

Bonus Trivia Quiz!

You think you are a true Cape Verde fan? Try this bonus quiz!

1. What is the capital city of Cape Verde?

A) Mindelo
B) Sal
C) Praia
D) Boa Vista

2. What nickname is used for the Cape Verde national team?

A) The Island Eagles
B) The Atlantic Lions
C) The Blue Sharks
D) The Ocean Kings

3. Which football confederation does Cape Verde compete in?

A) UEFA
B) AFC
C) CAF
D) CONCACAF

4. In what year did Cape Verde gain independence and later form its own national football identity?

A) 1968

B) 1975

C) 1982

D) 1990

5. What ocean surrounds the islands of Cape Verde?

A) Indian Ocean

B) Pacific Ocean

C) Southern Ocean

D) Atlantic Ocean

6. Which tournament did Cape Verde qualify for the first time in 2013?

A) FIFA World Cup

B) Africa Cup of Nations

C) African Nations Championship

D) Confederations Cup

7. In their first AFCON appearance in 2013, how far did Cape Verde advance?

A) Group stage

B) Round of 16

C) Quarterfinals

D) Final

8. Which team knocked Cape Verde out of AFCON 2013?

A) Nigeria

B) South Africa

C) Ghana

D) Morocco

9. What position did Bubista mainly play for Cape Verde?

A) Striker

B) Goalkeeper

C) Midfielder

D) Defender

10. Ryan Mendes became Cape Verde's all-time leader in what two categories?

A) Assists and trophies

B) Goals and club titles

C) Caps and goals

D) Matches and saves

11. A "cap" in football means what?

A) Winning a trophy

B) Playing one match for the national team

C) Scoring a goal

D) Wearing the captain's armband

12. Which island city is Ryan Mendes from?

A) Praia on Santiago

B) Mindelo on São Vicente

C) Sal on Sal

D) Assomada on Santiago

13. What do the ten yellow stars on Cape Verde's flag represent?

A) Past AFCON appearances

B) Famous players

C) Historic victories

D) The islands of the country

14. Why are home matches especially intense for Cape Verde?

A) The stadiums are very large

B) The crowd is far from the pitch

C) Fans are close, loud, and involved

D) Matches are always at night

15. What best describes Cape Verde's modern football mindset?

A) Careful and defensive

B) Nervous but hopeful

C) Calm, organized, and confident

D) Chaotic and emotional

Super Fan Secret Challenge

Only a true Cape Verde fan will know this.

(No Answer Provided)

- 88 -

Which Cape Verde defender was born in Portugal, chose to represent the islands, and became a long-time leader at the back during the team's rise?

A) Ryan Mendes

B) Fernando Varela

C) Babanco

D) Vozinha

Answer Key

1. C) Praia

2. C) The Blue Sharks

3. C) CAF

4. B) 1975

5. D) Atlantic Ocean

6. B) Africa Cup of Nations

7. C) Quarterfinals

8. C) Ghana

9. D) Defender

10. C) Caps and goals

11. B) Playing one match for the national team

12. B) Mindelo on São Vicente

13. D) The islands of the country

14. C) Fans are close, loud, and involved

15. C) Calm, organized, and confident

Fun Fan Facts:
The Unofficial World Cup Edition
Saudi Arabia
Everything Young Saudi Arabia Fans Should Know

By: Jake Liam

THE WORLD CUP
BY THE NUMBERS

MOST WORLD CUP WINS

Stars=Titles

★ ★ ★ ★ ★ BRAZIL

☆ ★ ★ ★ ★ GERMANY, ITALY

☆ ☆ ★ ★ ★ ARGENTINA

☆ ☆ ☆ ★ ★ FRANCE, URUGUAY

☆ ☆ ☆ ☆ ★ ENGLAND, SPAIN

GLOBAL REACH

5 BILLION
People Reached
(2022)

1.5 BILLION
Watched the
2022 Final

1930 TO TODAY

1930
1st World
Cup

1970
Pele's 3rd
Ttile

1982
Expands to
24 Teams

2022
Legendary
Final

48 | 8 | 22

Teams Competing in 2026 | **Countries Ever to Win It** | **World Cups Played***

* No World Cup was played in 1942 and 1946 due to World War II.
* 2026 will be the 23rd World Cup

WINNER BY YEAR

1930 – Uruguay
1934 – Italy
1938 – Italy
1950 – Uruguay
1954 – West Germany
1958 – Brazil
1962 – Brazil
1966 – England
1970 – Brazil
1974 – West Germany

1978 – Argentina
1982 – Italy
1986 – Argentina
1990 – West Germany
1994 – Brazil
1998 – France
2002 – Brazil
2006 – Italy
2010 – Spain
2014 – Germany
2018 – France
2022 – Argentina

SAUDI ARABIA
AT THE WORLD CUP

- FIRST PLAYED: 1994
- BEST FINISH: ROUND OF 16
  (1994)
- APPEARANCES: 6

19
Total Matches Played
in the World Cup

ALL-TIME MOST WORLD CUP GOALS

MIROSLAV KLOSE **(16)** ⚽ RONALDO NAZÁRIO **(15)** ⚽ GERD MÜLLER **(14)**

Saudi Arabia Facts

Capital

Riyadh

Population

about 37 million

National Sports

Football (soccer), camel racing, equestrian (horse
sports), falconry

Famous Foods

Kabsa, mandi, jareesh, mutabbaq

Region / Conference

Asia / AFC

Chapter 1: Where the Green Falcons Took Off

1. Why They're Called the Green Falcons

Saudi Arabia's national team nickname is the Green Falcons, and once you picture it, it makes perfect sense. Falcons are fast, focused, and deadly accurate. They also look cool doing literally anything. Add the color green from the national flag, and boom. Instant identity.

This nickname is not just about speed. Falcons are trained with patience and precision, and that matches how Saudi teams like to play when they are locked in. Calm buildup, sudden strike and the crowd goes wild.

Also, let's be honest. "Green Falcons" sounds like a team that already knows it is about to do something dramatic.

2. Football Gets Organized: The Federation Era Begins (1956)

Before 1956, football in Saudi Arabia was growing fast, but it was a little bit like pickup games with big dreams. Then the Saudi Arabian Football Federation was founded, and suddenly things got official. Rules, leagues, referees, schedules. This was the "okay, this is serious now" moment.

It mattered because a national team does not just appear out of nowhere. It gets built. Slowly. With planning, training, and a lot of matches where someone argues about whether that was offside.

From this point on, Saudi Arabia was not just playing football. They were building a football future.

3. Asia Qualifying: No Easy Roads Here

If you think qualifying for the World Cup is simple, Asia says, "Good luck with that." Long travel, different climates, packed stadiums, and teams that do not care about your feelings. Saudi Arabia grew up in that environment.

Playing in Asian qualifiers teaches teams how to survive. One week it is heat. Next week it is pressure.

Next week it is a must-win match where everyone back home is watching very closely.

That toughness became part of Saudi Arabia's football personality. When things get tense, they have been there before.

4. The Rise of the Big Clubs: Where the Talent Gets Loud

Saudi football fans know club football is where the fire really gets started. Teams like Al Hilal, Al Ittihad, and Al Nassr are not just clubs. They are weekly emotional roller coasters with jerseys. Rivalries get intense fast, and the stadium volume hits airplane-engine levels.

These clubs help build national team players the way a gym builds muscles: pressure, reps, and more pressure. Big crowds, big expectations, and the kind of match atmosphere where your first touch better be friendly, because the stands will definitely have an opinion.

By the time players reach the national team, they are already trained in the hardest skill of all: looking calm while 40,000 people collectively gasp at the same time.

5. Green Means Go: The Color That Takes Over Stadiums

Saudi Arabia's green shirts are impossible to miss. When the fans show up, it is not "a few people in green." It is a full green takeover. Flags, scarves, face paint, matching outfits, and at least one person waving something enormous like they are trying to signal a helicopter.

Green becomes more than a color. It becomes a warning sign for the other team: this match will be loud, and the Green Falcons are not landing quietly. The chant energy builds, the crowd starts bouncing, and suddenly the stadium feels like it has its own heartbeat.

Also, from a camera perspective, green looks amazing. It is like the team is sponsored by confidence.

6. Majed Abdullah: The Original Goal Machine (1977-1994)

Majed Abdullah grew up in Jeddah and became a star with Al-Nassr at a time when Saudi football was still building its identity. If Saudi Arabia had a "classic mode" football legend, it would be Majed Abdullah. He was the striker fans grew up hearing about like a family story: "Back in the day, Majed did not ask for chances. He collected them."

He had that pure goal scorer vibe. Calm in the box, sharp finishing, and the ability to turn a half-chance into a full celebration. The kind of player where defenders start backing up like, "Not again please."

To this day, his name still carries that "legend in the hallway" energy. Say it around fans and you will see the nod. Respect.

7. Sami Al-Jaber: Mr. World Cup Era (1994-2006)

Sami Al-Jaber is the kind of player who feels like he was always there, because he basically was. A product of Al-Hilal, Sami Al-Jaber rose through Saudi football just as the national team began appearing regularly on the world stage. He played across multiple World Cup eras for Saudi Arabia, which is a big deal because World Cups are spaced far apart. That means longevity, consistency, and a body that apparently never got the memo about needing rest.

Fans remember him as a symbol of Saudi Arabia staying on the global stage. When the team needed calm leadership and a player who understood the moment, Al-Jaber was that guy.

Also, imagine being in a squad where people are nervous, and one teammate is like, "Relax. I've done this before." Instant confidence boost.

8. Yasser Al-Qahtani: The Star with the Smile (2002-2013)

Yasser Al-Qahtani brought modern-star energy. He could score, create, and carry that "I am not panicking" look even when the match was doing cartwheels. Yasser Al-Qahtani emerged from the Eastern Province and became the face of Al-Hilal during a new, more modern Saudi football era. He had the kind of presence where fans lean forward because something clever might happen.

He also became one of those players casual fans recognize fast. You might not know every roster, but you know the name. That is a legend marker.

And yes, he had that fan-favorite power: making difficult things look like they were part of the plan all along.

9. Mohammed Al-Deayea: The Goalkeeper With the Steel Nerves (1993-2006)

Born in Ha'il and trusted for years between the posts for Al-Hilal, Mohammed Al-Deayea became the calm constant behind Saudi Arabia's biggest matches.

Goalkeepers live a weird life. They can be perfect for 89 minutes, and then one moment happens and everyone forgets the other 89. Mohammed Al-Deayea handled that pressure for years, which tells you everything you need to know about his nerve level.

He became a cornerstone for Saudi Arabia, the kind of keeper who made attackers second-guess shots. Not because he was loud, but because he was ready.

A great goalkeeper is basically a human "not today" sign. Al-Deayea wore that sign proudly.

10. Salem Al-Dawsari: The Big-Moment Left Foot (2012-present)

A Riyadh-born winger who came through Al-Hilal, Salem Al-Dawsari represents the generation raised expecting Saudi Arabia to compete. Some players are built for normal matches. Salem Al-Dawsari is built for moments when the whole world is watching. He has flair, confidence, and a left foot that loves drama, especially the good kind.

When he gets space, fans get that feeling like, "Uh-oh for the other team." One touch, quick shift, and suddenly the ball is traveling like it has somewhere important to be.

He is the type of player who can change a match and then celebrate like, "Yes, I meant that." Because he did.

Chapter 3: Moments That Made the World Look Twice

11. World Cup Debut and Zero Fear Energy (1994)

Saudi Arabia's first ever World Cup appearance came in 1994, and the vibe was not "happy to be here." It was "hi everyone, please notice us." Debut tournaments are supposed to be cautious. Saudi Arabia skipped that memo entirely.

They played with confidence, speed, and zero nerves, like a team that had already decided this stage belonged to them too. Fans around the world learned quickly that this was not a filler team. This was a team with ideas.

First impression locked in. It was loud.

12. The Belgium Win That Turned Heads (1994)

Facing Belgium at the 1994 World Cup was a serious test. Belgium had experience, history, and expectations. Saudi Arabia had belief, energy, and absolutely no plans to sit back politely.

The result was a 1 - 0, a Saudi win that made commentators sit up straighter. We'll get back to that one goal in a minute. This was one of those games where the underdog script gets flipped, folded, and thrown out the window.

From that moment on, teams stopped seeing Saudi Arabia as "new." They saw them as "dangerous."

13. Saeed Al-Owairan's Run: The Goal Against Belgium (1994)

Now, back to the goal against Belgium. The moment came during the 1994 World Cup group-stage match against, with Saudi Arabia needing something special to keep their tournament alive. Saeed Al-Owairan picked up the ball deep in his own half, turned, and decided this was his moment. He ran. Past one defender. Then another. Then another. It stopped being a normal attack and turned into something unreal.

Belgium scrambled to recover. The pitch seemed to stretch as Al-Owairan kept gliding forward, the ball glued to his feet. By the time he reached the box and finished calmly into the net, it felt like he had sprinted through the entire stadium. One run. One goal. Total silence. Then chaos.

Saudi Arabia won the match 1 - 0, a result that sent them through to the knockout stage for the first time in their history. The goal was replayed around the world, earning Al-Owairan the legendary nickname: 'The Maradona of the Desert.' It wasn't just compared to the greatest solo goals ever scored; it became one of them. Not just a highlight. Not just a win. It was Saudi Arabia announcing itself on football's biggest stage, at full speed, with no intention of slowing down.

14. Group Stage Equals Knockouts: Welcome to the Round of 16 (1994)

At the 1994 World Cup, the group stage decided who reached the Round of 16, the knockout phase where one loss sends you home. Saudi Arabia finished second in their group, which meant they advanced straight into elimination football.

That matters because this was Saudi Arabia's first-ever World Cup, and they were already playing with no safety net. No practice run. Just win or pack your bags. Saudi Arabia's knockout run ended in the Round of 16 against Sweden, a 3 - 1 loss, which meant the debut adventure was over the moment the whistle blew.

Making the Round of 16 in a debut tournament sent a clear message: Saudi Arabia was not just visiting the World Cup. They were competing in it.

15. The Argentina Shock That Broke the Internet (2022)

Fast-forward to 2022, and Saudi Arabia walked into a World Cup group match against Argentina, one of the tournament favorites, packed with stars and expectations. The script was already written. Saudi Arabia ignored it.

After going down early, the Green Falcons came back and won 2 - 1. Goals, discipline, fearless defending, and a defensive line pushed so high it felt like the game was happening right on the halfway line. When the final whistle blew, social media exploded. Memes. Replays. Respect.

It was a reminder that Saudi Arabia does not need permission to make history. They just do it.

16. Yalla Ya Akhdar: The Chant That Shakes Buildings

Every team has a chant. Saudi Arabia has a full-volume announcement. "Yalla Ya Akhdar!" means "Let's go, Green," and when it starts rolling through a stadium, it does not ask politely. It arrives.

The chant builds in layers. One section starts it. Another answers. Then suddenly the whole place is bouncing like the stadium just remembered it has knees. Players hear it. Opponents definitely hear it. Nearby cities probably hear it too.

It is not just noise. It is belief with rhythm. The kind that says, "You are not alone out there. We brought backup."

17. Green Everywhere: When Match Day Becomes a Color Explosion

On Saudi match days, green is not a suggestion. It is a rule. Shirts, scarves, flags, face paint, hats, capes, and at least one person wrapped like a human flag who is having the best day of their life.

When thousands of fans show up dressed the same color, it turns the stands into a moving wave. Cameras love it. Players feel it. The other team definitely notices it during warm-ups.

It is like the crowd is saying, "We dressed for the occasion. Hope you did too."

18. Riyadh and Jeddah Nights: When the Cities Join the Match

In cities like Riyadh and Jeddah, big matches do not stay inside the stadium. Cafes fill up. Screens appear everywhere. Cars honk in celebration. Someone's uncle becomes the unofficial referee from his chair.

When Saudi Arabia scores, the reaction travels fast. Cheers spill into the streets, group chats explode, and strangers start high-fiving like they have known each other for years. Football turns into a shared language.

For those nights, the whole city feels like one giant living room watching the same screen.

19. Match Day Hospitality: Coffee, Dates, and Football Debates

Watching football in Saudi Arabia often comes with hospitality built in. Arabic coffee, dates, snacks, and a seat that someone insists you take, even if you say you are fine standing. That is not optional.

The game plays, the coffee pours, and debates start immediately. Was that offside. Should he have passed. Who saw that run. These conversations can last longer than the match itself and are taken very seriously.

Basically, football plus hospitality equals a gathering that accidentally becomes a tradition.

20. More Than Football: Falcons, Camels, and Sporting Roots

Football is the headline act, but Saudi sports culture runs deeper. Falconry and camel racing are traditional sports that value patience, training, and respect. Those ideas carry over into football too.

Falcons are trained carefully, not rushed. Camels are prepared over time, not overnight. That same mindset shows up in how players are developed and supported. Growth matters. Process matters.

So when the Green Falcons fly on the pitch, they are carrying more than tactics. They are carrying tradition.

21. The League Glow-Up: When the Spotlight Got Brighter

Saudi football has always mattered at home, but lately it has been louder on the world stage too. Big-name players arriving in the league turned casual scrolling into "wait, that match is on tonight?" energy. Suddenly more eyes are watching, more cameras are rolling, and the pressure level goes up for everyone.

For Saudi players, that can be a cheat code and a challenge at the same time. Training gets sharper. Standards get higher. Young players get to learn up close from people who have played on the biggest stages.

Also, it makes local fans feel like the football universe moved a little closer to home. Like the world came to visit, and Saudi football said, "Welcome. Now try to keep up."

22. Youth Development: The Next Falcons Are Already Running

Every national team future starts with kids playing everywhere, then getting better coaching, better training, better chances. Saudi Arabia has been putting more focus on developing young players, building systems that help talent grow instead of getting lost.

The funny thing about future stars is you can spot them early, because they do the same two things. One, they ask for the ball in the scariest moments. Two, they try something bold and then look surprised when it works.

Somewhere right now, a kid is practicing a free kick and thinking, "This one is for the World Cup." No pressure. Just a casual dream.

23. Stadiums and Hosting Energy: Building Big Stages

Saudi Arabia has been investing in new stadiums and big sports events, and that matters because facilities change what is possible. Better pitches, better training spaces, bigger crowds, and more major matches hosted at home.

When a country builds stadiums, it is not just about seats. It is about creating a place where memories happen. The kind of place where a kid goes to one match, hears the roar, and suddenly decides, "Yep. I'm doing this for real."

Also, modern stadium lights have a special power. They make everything look like a final, even if it is a Tuesday.

24. The 2026 Target: Back to the Biggest Stage

World Cup qualifying is not a straight road. It is more like a maze where every corner has a new test. Saudi Arabia's goal is simple: get back to the World Cup and make noise, not just attendance.

And the Green Falcons have something that always helps in qualifying. Belief. Fans who bring energy everywhere. Players who know that one big win can flip the whole story.

The best part of a World Cup push is the "any moment can become history" feeling. One goal can turn into a lifetime highlight.

25. The Next Icon Moment: Someone Is About to Become a Household Name

This is my favorite kind of prediction because it is guaranteed to happen, but nobody knows exactly who it will be. At some point, a Saudi player will have a match where everything clicks. A big goal. A big assist. A big save. A big moment. Suddenly the world learns the name.

That is how football works. Legends do not get announced. They get revealed. One scene at a time.

If you are watching Saudi Arabia and you see a young player doing brave things, remember this: you might be watching the beginning of the next story fans tell forever. Yes, you are allowed to say, "I knew it," even if you only knew it five minutes ago. That's the future. The Green Falcons are still flying, and the next plot twist is already warming up on the sideline.

Saudi Arabia at the 2022 World Cup, standing there like, "Yes, we are calm. Yes, we are focused. Yes, something dramatic is absolutely about to happen." National shirts on, game faces locked, plot twist loading. *Photo by Tasnim News Agency, Saudi National Team at the World Cup 2022, via Wikimedia Commons, licensed under Creative Commons Attribution 4.0.*

Bonus Trivia Quiz!

You think you are a true Saudi Arabia fan? Try this bonus quiz!

1. When did Saudi Arabia play their first widely listed official international matches (at the Pan-Arab Games in Beirut)?

A) 1948
B) 1952
C) 1957
D) 1966

2. What is Saudi Arabia's national team nickname?

A) The Desert Kings
B) The Green Falcons
C) The Palm Warriors
D) The Red Knights

3. What is the capital of Saudi Arabia?

A) Jeddah
B) Riyadh
C) Dammam
D) Mecca

4. Saudi Arabia is part of which football confederation?

A) UEFA

B) CONMEBOL

C) AFC

D) CAF

5. What does the chant "Yalla Ya Akhdar" mean in match-day spirit?

A) Let's go, Green

B) We love extra time

C) Pass the snacks

D) Ref, please listen

6. In which year did Saudi Arabia make their men's World Cup debut?

A) 1982

B) 1990

C) 1994

D) 2002

7. Which team did Saudi Arabia beat 1-0 at the 1994 World Cup in the match famous for Saeed Al-Owairan's solo run?

A) Morocco
B) Belgium
C) Netherlands
D) Sweden

8. What was special about Al-Owairan's famous 1994 goal (the vibe, not the physics homework)?

A) A long solo dribble through multiple defenders
B) A header from the halfway line
C) A bicycle kick from a corner
D) A penalty taken with his back to goal

9. Reaching the Round of 16 means what at the World Cup?

A) You are in the knockout stage
B) You won the trophy
C) You skip the group stage
D) You only play friendly matches

10. In 2022, Saudi Arabia shocked the world by beating which tournament favorite in their group opener?

A) France

B) Brazil

C) Argentina

D) Germany

11. What was the final score of that Saudi Arabia vs Argentina match at the 2022 World Cup?

A) 1-0

B) 2-1

C) 3-2

D) 4-3

12. Which two Saudi players scored the goals in the 2-1 win over Argentina in 2022?

A) Salem Al-Dawsari and Saleh Al-Shehri

B) Majed Abdullah and Sami Al-Jaber

C) Yasser Al-Qahtani and Mohammed Al-Deayea

D) None, it was all own goals

13. Which position is Mohammed Al-Deayea most known for?

A) Goalkeeper
B) Striker
C) Left back
D) Referee

14. FC Metz is a club in France. Ligue 1 is what?

A) France's highest professional league
B) France's second division
C) A stadium in Paris
D) A trophy for best fans

15. Which color is the signature color of Saudi Arabia's national team look and fan wave?

A) Blue
B) Green
C) Purple
D) Orange

Super Fan Secret Challenge

Only a true Saudi Arabia fan will know this.

(No Answer Provided)

- 125 -

In which city and stadium did Saudi Arabia's 1994 "Al-Owairan wonder goal" match against Belgium take place?

A) Washington, D.C., RFK Stadium

B) New York City, Yankee Stadium

C) Los Angeles, Rose Bowl

D) Miami, Hard Rock Stadium

Answer Key

1. C) 1957

2. B) The Green Falcons

3. B) Riyadh

4. C) AFC

5. A) Let's go, Green

6. C) 1994

7. B) Belgium

8. A) A long solo dribble through multiple defenders

9. A) You are in the knockout stage

10. C) Argentina

11. B) 2-1

12. A) Salem Al-Dawsari and Saleh Al-Shehri

13. A) Goalkeeper

14. A) France's highest professional league

15. B) Green

Fun Fan Facts:
The Unofficial World Cup Edition

Uruguay

Everything Young Uruguay Fans Should Know

By: Jake Liam

THE WORLD CUP
BY THE NUMBERS

MOST WORLD CUP WINS

Stars=Titles

★ ★ ★ ★ ★ BRAZIL

☆ ★ ★ ★ ★ GERMANY, ITALY

☆ ☆ ★ ★ ★ ARGENTINA

☆ ☆ ☆ ★ ★ FRANCE, URUGUAY

☆ ☆ ☆ ☆ ★ ENGLAND, SPAIN

GLOBAL REACH

5 BILLION
People Reached (2022)

1.5 BILLION
Watched the 2022 Final

1930 TO TODAY

1930 — 1st World Cup

1970 — Pele's 3rd Ttile

1982 — Expands to 24 Teams

2022 — Legendary Final

48 | 8 | 22

48 Teams Competing in 2026

8 Countries Ever to Win It

22 World Cups Played*

No World Cup was played in 1942 and 1946 due to World War II.

2026 will be the 23rd World Cup

WINNER BY YEAR

1930 – Uruguay
1934 – Italy
1938 – Italy
1950 – Uruguay
1954 – West Germany
1958 – Brazil
1962 – Brazil
1966 – England
1970 – Brazil
1974 – West Germany

1978 – Argentina
1982 – Italy
1986 – Argentina
1990 – West Germany
1994 – Brazil
1998 – France
2002 – Brazil
2006 – Italy
2010 – Spain
2014 – Germany
2018 – France
2022 – Argentina

URUGUAY
AT THE WORLD CUP

- FIRST PLAYED: 1930
- WINNER: 2 TIMES (1930, 1950)
- APPEARANCES: 14

8-0 Biggest Win Vs. Bolivia (1950)

ALL-TIME MOST WORLD CUP GOALS

MIROSLAV KLOSE **(16)** ⚽ RONALDO NAZÁRIO **(15)** ⚽ GERD MÜLLER **(14)**

Uruguay Facts

Capital

Montevideo

Population

about 3.4 million

National Sports

football, basketball and rugby

Famous Food

chivito, asado

Region / Conference

South America / CONMEBOL

Chapter 1: Where World Football Began

1. Football Finds a Home in Montevideo

Picture Montevideo in the late 1800s. It is a busy port city with ships coming in, workers heading to rail yards, and students learning new games at schools tied to British communities. Football shows up early, and people do not treat it like a random hobby. They treat it like a new language. One of the earliest recorded club matches in Uruguay was played in 1881, and by 1891 Montevideo had a real football club called Albion, started by students connected to the English High School. Around the same time, railway workers formed CURCC, a club that would later connect to the story of Peñarol. Suddenly, football is not "a thing some visitors do." It is a thing the city starts owning.

Then the passion gets organized. In 1900, Uruguay's clubs help form a national league organization (the AUF), and now the games have schedules, trophies, and real bragging rights. Montevideo becomes a football engine: neighborhoods, schools, and workplaces all feeding into teams. That is how it starts in Uruguay. Not with one magic moment, but with a city deciding, together, that the ball matters.

2. A Nation Built Around the Ball

Uruguay is squeezed between two football giants, Brazil and Argentina, with a population smaller than many cities. That could have made the country feel tiny. Instead, football became Uruguay's megaphone to shout, "We're here, and we're not backing down!"

In Montevideo, clubs aren't just teams. They're neighborhoods with a pulse. Colors run deep. Songs echo for generations. Picking a side, like Peñarol or Nacional, becomes family legend. Match day? Streets flood with flags, friends, and pure noise. It's like the whole city picks up a heartbeat and marches to the stadium.

Then Uruguay started winning big, and early. That lit the fire. When a small nation beats the giants on the world stage, kids grow up thinking bravery is everyday stuff. Success isn't a fluke. It's the expectation. Not easy wins, fearless fights.

That's why football is Uruguay's soul. It's the loudest way to say, "We belong," no matter how strong the opponent looks. The second the whistle blows, that attitude explodes onto the pitch. Garra Charrúa: pure Uruguayan fight!

3. Olympic Glory Before the World Cup

Before there was a World Cup trophy to chase, the Olympics were basically football's biggest international stage. So, when Uruguay traveled to Paris in 1924, they were not just showing up for a nice vacation and a few matches. They were arriving to prove a point. European crowds had not seen football played quite like this: quick passes, clever movement, and a calm confidence that made it look like the ball was on a string. Uruguay won the gold medal, and suddenly people outside South America were whispering the same sentence: Who are these guys?

Then Uruguay did the funniest, boldest thing possible. They repeated it. In 1928, they went to Amsterdam and won Olympic gold again. Back-to-back. That kind of success does something powerful to a country's mindset. It turns hope into expectation. It turns "maybe we can" into "we will fight for it every time." By the time the first World Cup was being planned for 1930, Uruguay was not acting like a newcomer to big moments. They were acting like a team that had already lived there, unpacked their bags, and hung their coat on the hook.

4. Two Stars Are Born

Uruguay's rise to the top did not happen in slow motion. It happened with trophies. Before the World Cup even existed, Uruguay went to the Olympics and started turning heads. In 1924, they won Olympic gold and made the football world stop and stare. Then they did it again in 1928. Back-to-back. That is the moment Uruguay stopped feeling like a cute underdog story and started feeling like a football problem everyone had to solve.

Now look at the crest. Four stars. And yes, they mean something. Two are for those Olympic titles in 1924 and 1928, back when Olympic football was the biggest international prize around. The other two are for the World Cups in 1930 and 1950. So the stars are basically a timeline you can wear. It says, plain and simple: Uruguay was winning before the world even named the biggest tournament. And they never stopped believing they belonged at the top.

5. Small Population, Big Belief

Uruguay has about 3.4 million people. That is smaller than a lot of cities. So, if football talent worked like a giant vending machine, Uruguay should be out of snacks by halftime. But Uruguay does not run on numbers. It runs on belief. In small towns and big neighborhoods, the game feels personal, like everyone has a cousin who plays, a grandparent with a story, and a coach who will happily give you advice even if you did not ask.

And the proof is in the trophies. Uruguay has won the Copa América 15 times, which is absolutely wild for a country this size. That kind of history turns pressure into normal weather. It teaches players to treat big moments like, "Yep, this is what we do." So when Uruguay lines up against a giant, nobody's thinking, "We're small." They're thinking, "Good. Let's make this interesting."

6. The Magician: Héctor Scarone (1917-1930)

If Uruguay's early golden era was a superhero team, Héctor Scarone was the one doing tricks with the cape on. He grew up in Montevideo, the capital of Uruguay, at a time when the country was just beginning to shock the football world. Fans called him El Mago, which means The Magician, because the ball seemed to follow his feet like it had a crush. He played for Nacional, starred for Uruguay, and lined up as an inside forward, basically a crafty attacker who creates chances and finishes them too. In the 1920s, that role was like being the team's idea machine and the team's closer at the same time.

Scarone's timing was perfect, and so was his trophy collection. He was part of the Uruguay sides that won Olympic gold in 1924 and 1928, then helped them win the first World Cup in 1930. That is three giant titles in the era when Uruguay was teaching the rest of the world to take them seriously. He also scored 31 goals for the national team, which stood as Uruguay's record for years. Tiny country, big magic, and Scarone was right in the middle of the spell.

7. The Chief: Obdulio Varela (1939-1954)

If Héctor Scarone was Uruguay's magic, Obdulio Varela was the voice that makes everyone stand up straighter. Born in Montevideo and shaped by hard streets and harder matches, Varela represented the gritty side of Uruguayan football. He played midfield, the part of the field where games get decided in messy, crowded moments, and he did it like a captain in a storm. In Uruguay, he was known as El Jefe, meaning The Chief, because when things got tense, he did not flinch. He slowed the game down when it needed calm, and he cranked it up when it needed courage. Not fancy. Not loud for attention. Just fearless.

And then came 1950. The World Cup final round ended with Uruguay facing Brazil in the Maracanã, a massive stadium in Brazil packed with nearly 200,000 fans: a crowd so huge it sounded like the stadium had its own weather system. Brazil scored first. The pressure got heavy fast. Varela did something legendary: he refused to let panic win a single second. He argued the goal, took his time, walked, talked, steadied everyone, and basically stole the crowd's momentum with pure nerve. Uruguay came back, won 2 to 1, and shocked the world. That is why Varela is not just a player in Uruguay's history. He is a symbol of it.

8. The Prince: Enzo Francescoli (1982-1997)

Some players fight the game. Enzo Francescoli floated
through it. He came from Montevideo too, but his
football felt international, elegant, and almost
effortless. Fans called him El Príncipe, The Prince,
because he played like he was wearing a cape you could
not see. One touch, calm. One turn, gone. One pass,
and suddenly the whole defense is pointing at each
other like, "Wait, whose job was that?" He was the kind
of attacker who made hard things look smooth, and in
Uruguay, smooth is not a bonus. Smooth is bravery with
good posture.

And here's the part that makes your brain do a little
backflip. A kid in France watched Francescoli and
basically decided, "Yep. That's my favorite player on
Earth." That kid was Zinedine Zidane. Years later, Zidane
named his son Enzo because he admired Francescoli
that much. Imagine being so cool at football that
another future legend uses your name for their kid.
That is next-level respect.

Francescoli also gave Uruguay something huge in the
1980s and 1990s: belief with style. When the sky blue
shirt needed a leader who could inspire without yelling,

The Prince showed up, head up, chest out, and made the game feel possible again.

9. Cachavacha: Diego Forlán (2002-2014)

If Uruguay's nickname squad needed someone who could change a game with one swing of the boot, it was Diego Forlán. Born into a football family in Montevideo and tested across Europe's toughest leagues, Forlán brought Uruguay back into the modern spotlight. His nickname was Cachavacha, like the cartoon witch, and it fits because his shots felt like spells. One second the ball is way out there, minding its business, and the next second it is screaming into the net like it just got launched by a slingshot. Forlán was not just a striker waiting for tap-ins. He could score from distance, hit free kicks, and punish teams the moment they got a little too comfortable.

Then came 2010, the tournament that turned him into a full-blown national icon. Uruguay made a deep run, and Forlán was the face of it: goals, leadership, and that calm, "give me the ball" confidence when everything got tight. He won the Golden Ball as the best player of the World Cup, which is basically football's way of saying, "Yep, that guy was the main character." He gave

Uruguay modern magic that still felt old-school, the kind built on guts, work, and big moments. Witch nickname or not, Forlán's real power was simple: he made Uruguay believe they belonged in the late stages of the biggest tournament on Earth.

10. The Pistolero: Luis Suárez (2007--Present)

Luis Suárez is the kind of striker who makes defenders feel like they are babysitting a firework. Raised in Salto, a smaller city far from the capital, Suárez played with the hunger of someone who knew nothing would be handed to him. His nickname is El Pistolero, The Gunman, and it fits because his shots show up fast and loud. For Uruguay, he was not just a scorer. He was a spark. He finished chances that looked impossible, celebrated like the whole country was in his chest, and played with the attitude of a kid who refuses to lose a backyard game, even if the backyard is a World Cup stadium.

He also came with edge. Sometimes that edge helped Uruguay survive the biggest moments, like the famous 2010 quarterfinal against Ghana, when he made a last second choice that turned him into the most talked about player on Earth. Sometimes that edge crossed the line, and things got awkward fast, including an infamous biting incident at the 2014 World Cup. That is Suárez in a nutshell: genius, chaos, headlines, goals.

He delivered. He helped Uruguay win Copa América in 2011, and he finished his international career as Uruguay's all-time top scorer with 69 goals. Love him, gasp at him, argue about him, you still have to admit it: when El Pistolero showed up, the game got dangerous.

And when you call roll, the whole squad makes sense. The Magician created it, The Chief protected it, The Prince polished it, Cachavacha cast the long-range spell, and The Pistolero finished it with a grin that basically says, "Go on then. Bite me."

11. Hosting and Winning the First Ever World Cup

Montevideo in 1930 was buzzing like a carnival that just happened to include football history. The air on match day carried salty sea breeze from the port, grilled meat smoke from street vendors, and the sharp smell of fresh-cut grass from the stadium. Uruguay was not just hosting the first World Cup. They were inviting the world into their living room and saying, "Welcome. Shoes off. We're playing."

The tournament was small by today's standards with 13 teams, but it felt enormous because nobody had ever done this before. Then Uruguay went and won it. In the final on July 30, 1930, at the Estadio Centenario, they beat Argentina 4 to 2. And that mattered forever. The first champions were not a giant empire or a country with endless numbers. It was Uruguay, a small nation with huge belief, showing the world that courage and craft could rule the biggest stage, even when the stage was brand new.

12. The Maracanazo of 1950

July 16, 1950. Rio de Janeiro. Brazil's Maracanã stadium was packed so full it felt like the stadium could barely breathe. Brazil only needed a draw to win the World Cup, and the crowd came ready to celebrate before the game was even finished. You could almost hear the victory party warming up. Then Uruguay walked out in sky blue and acted like the noise was just background music. Their captain, Obdulio Varela, kept everyone calm, like he had a remote control for panic.

Brazil scored first early in the second half and the place exploded. That should have been the cue for a small team to wobble. Uruguay did the opposite. Juan Alberto Schiaffino tied it, and suddenly the roar turned into nervous murmuring. Then came the moment that became a legend: Alcides Ghiggia scored to make it 2 to 1 for Uruguay. The ball hit the net, and the Maracanã did something nobody expected. It went quiet. Not polite quiet. Shock quiet. Like someone pressed mute on the stadium.

That is why people call it the Maracanazo, basically "the Maracanã punch." Uruguay did not just win a match. They stole a whole ending that the world thought was already written. In one afternoon, a tiny nation reminded everyone of football's biggest rule: the game does not care what the crowd believes. It only cares what you do next.

1950 World Cup final round showdown at the Maracanã in Rio de Janeiro: Juan Alberto Schiaffino slams in the equalizer to make it 1 to 1. One net ripple and the whole stadium goes from "party planning" to "wait... what?" This was the spark right before Uruguay landed the punch that clinched the title. *Photo credit: El Gráfico (photographer unknown), public domain, via Wikimedia Common*

13. Winning With Courage, Not Comfort

Uruguay has never needed perfect conditions to play brave football. Give them a muddy pitch, a loud crowd, a long trip, and an opponent with bigger names, and they do not ask for upgrades. They just tighten their laces and go. Part of that is history. When your country is small, you learn early that waiting for everything to feel "ideal" is a trap. So Uruguay built a reputation on doing the hard stuff first: tackling, tracking back, fighting for second balls (those loose rebounds nobody owns yet), and staying organized when the game gets chaotic.

But courage is not just crashing into tackles. Uruguay's best teams also had the nerve to stay calm and smart when everyone else got jumpy. They could win without comfort by believing they belonged in the moment. That belief is the real weapon. It turns pressure into focus. It turns noise into background. It turns "we're supposed to lose" into "watch this." And that is why Uruguay's biggest wins feel like more than wins. They feel like proof that fearlessness is a style of football, not just a mood.

14. Forlán's 2010 Run to Fourth

Roll call, because this is where the nickname squad time-travels into the modern era. In 2010, Uruguay landed in South Africa and started playing like the old stories were alive again. Tight games. Enormous nerves. No shortcuts. Uruguay reached the World Cup semifinals for the first time since 1970, and Diego Forlán was the face of it. He scored five goals, kept showing up in the tensest minutes, and played with that calm look that says, "Yep. I can handle this." He even won the Golden Ball as the tournament's best player, which is football's way of handing you the "main character" badge.

And the run had drama stacked on drama. A quarterfinal that went to penalties. A semifinal loss to the Netherlands, 3 to 2, where Uruguay fought right to the end. Then an absolute thriller against Germany for third place, another 3 to 2, with Forlán blasting shots that swerved like a knuckleball (that is when the ball wobbles in the air like it cannot decide where to go). Uruguay finished fourth, but the feeling was bigger than a number. It felt like history tapping the microphone and saying, "Still here."

15. Modern Tournaments, Old Spirit

Some countries have "eras." Uruguay has echoes. Even when the names change, the vibe shows up again like a familiar song you did not realize you knew by heart. You see it in how they defend like every inch matters. You see it in how they treat tense minutes like a place they've visited before. And you definitely see it in how Uruguay never acts impressed by an opponent's reputation. Big name? Big stadium? Big crowd? Uruguay's response is basically: cool. Let's play.

After 2010, the proof kept coming. In 2011, Uruguay won the Copa América again and reminded everyone they are not just a World Cup memory. They reload. New leaders step up. New kids grow up fast. And the old spirit keeps popping up at the exact moment a game gets tight, like history leaning over the touchline and whispering, "You know what to do." That's Uruguay. They do not frame their legacy. They bring it with them.

Chapter 4: Garra Charrúa

16. What Garra Charrúa Means

Garra Charrúa is Uruguay's secret ingredient, and it is not something you can measure with a stopwatch. Garra means "claw," like a team that refuses to let go. Charrúa points back to the Indigenous Charrúa people, a name that Uruguayans later connected to toughness and pride. Put it together and you get the idea fans love most: fight with your whole heart, protect your badge, and keep going even when your legs are begging for a break. It is not just "try hard." It is "we are still here."

Now, where did the phrase come from exactly? That part gets a little foggy. Some say it grew over time in newspapers and football talk, turning into a national slogan little by little. Others tie it to specific eras when Uruguay kept shocking bigger teams and needed a name for that stubborn bravery. Either way, the meaning is crystal clear when you watch Uruguay in a tight match. Shirts get tugged. Socks get muddy. Players throw themselves into blocks like the goal is a family heirloom.

Garra Charrúa is also a promise to the fans. You do not have to win every game. But you do have to show your teeth. Not rude teeth. Determined teeth.

17. Sky Blue as a Symbol

Uruguay's shirt is called La Celeste. It sounds simple, but it feels like a title. That sky blue looks calm, almost gentle, until you remember what it has seen. Trophies. Nerves. Stadiums that went silent. When Uruguay walks out in that color, it is like carrying history on your shoulders, except the history is cheering you on.

And the shirt does something to the player wearing it. You can be a teenager making your first appearance, knees a little shaky, and then you pull on La Celeste and you are suddenly part of a long line. Scarone. Varela. Francescoli. Forlán. Suárez. Roll call. Fans see the color and they expect a certain kind of football: brave defending, smart choices, and zero fear of famous names. The jersey is a reminder that Uruguay does not borrow confidence. They bring their own.

18. Fans Who Expect Bravery

In Uruguay, fans do not come to be entertained. They come to measure courage. Miss a chance, fine. Lose a match, it happens. But if you stop running, stop fighting for loose balls, or look like you are hiding from the moment, the crowd will notice fast. The deal is simple: wear La Celeste and show your spine.

And they bring their culture with them. At the Estadio Centenario, the stadium itself is a monument to Uruguay's football history, and there's even a museum inside. So the past is not far away. It is literally in the building. Add the drums, the songs, and the mate cups in the stands, and you get a crowd that feels like a family and a final exam at the same time. They will lift you. They will also demand you earn it.

19. Playing on the Edge

Picture it. A tight match, late minutes, sweat in your eyes, and the air feels heavy like it is holding its breath. Uruguay is down your throat. Not reckless, organized. The back line stays compact. The midfield snaps into challenges. Every loose ball turns into a race, and Uruguay runs it like it's the last slice of pizza.

And there's an attitude you can feel. A little shoulder-to-shoulder. A teammate sliding in fast, then popping up like nothing happened. A stare that says, "We're still here." It's not about backing away. It's about living in the uncomfortable moments and looking totally at home.

20. Respect Earned Through Battle

Uruguay's reputation was not built with shiny promises. It was built with muddy socks, scraped knees, and scorelines that made people blink twice. Over and over, they showed the same habit: when the moment gets uncomfortable, Uruguay gets comfortable. They do not win everyone's hearts with fancy tricks. They win respect with nerve.

Ask opponents what it feels like and you get the same picture. Every pass feels contested. Every late minute feels dangerous. Uruguay will fight for a draw like it is a trophy and chase a win like it is personal. That is why teams never relax against them. You do not play Uruguay and think, "This will be easy." You play Uruguay and think, "Okay. Helmets on."

Chapter 5: Carrying the Weight of History

21. New Generations, Same Demands

Imagine you're a teenager walking into the stadium tunnel for the first time in La Celeste. The air is cool and echoey, and everything smells like fresh grass, tape, and that clean "new jersey" fabric. You can hear drums thumping somewhere above, like the stands have a heartbeat. Your boots tap on the floor. Your stomach does a little flip. Then you look up and see the older players ahead of you, calm faces, same sky blue, like they've been here a thousand times. In Uruguay, your debut is not only a moment. It's a handoff.

Because the standard does not change just because the name on the back is new. Fans might not demand perfection, but they do demand bravery. Win your duel. Chase the loose ball. Get up fast. Help your teammate. If you do that, the crowd is with you. If you don't, it gets quiet in a way you can feel. That's how Uruguay keeps reloading. New generations show up, but the message stays the same: you're not wearing a shirt. You're joining a story.

22. Youth Development with Teeth

In Uruguay, football doesn't start with fancy stadium lights. It starts on small fields with bumpy grass, scuffed cones, and kids who play like the ball is a secret they have to protect. That's baby fútbol, where you learn the basics fast: first touch, quick passing, and how to keep going when you get bumped and the game keeps moving. No drama. Just play.

And here's the key. Those kids grow up hearing the same message as the legends: be brave when it gets tight. So, pressure stops feeling scary and starts feeling familiar. By the time a young player walks into a real stadium tunnel in La Celeste, it's not a brand-new world. It's the same test, just louder.

23. Competing Against Giants Again

Uruguay is the classic contrast team. Small country, huge expectations. Quiet population, loud football. Sky blue shirts that look gentle, and a style that feels like sandpaper. They line up against giants with deeper benches, bigger leagues, and more headlines, and somehow Uruguay still looks like they belong in the same room. Not by pretending. By competing.

And they keep proving it in modern eras. New faces come through, the pressure stays the same, and Uruguay still finds ways to punch above their weight. They might not always have the flashiest stars or the smoothest path, but they bring something opponents hate dealing with: belief that does not wobble. When the match gets tight and everyone starts thinking about consequences, Uruguay starts thinking about opportunities.

24. Legacy as Motivation, Not Burden

Let's be honest. Some of Uruguay's stars come from a long time ago. The first ones were earned in the 1920s, and the World Cup wins were 1930 and 1950. That is almost a century back. So you might think the history would feel dusty, like an old trophy on a high shelf.

But that is not how Uruguay wears it. They carry it like a battery. The stories are not there to make players nervous. They are there to make players bold. In Uruguay, history is not a reminder of what you cannot live up to. It's a reminder of what is possible when you refuse to blink. That is why, even now, teams still look at La Celeste and think, "Yep. These guys again."

25. Always Dangerous

In a World Cup knockout game, nobody wants to see Uruguay on the other side of the bracket. Not because they always have the most famous squad, but because they turn tournaments into survival stories. One goal up, they lock in. One goal down, they crank the pressure. And if it goes late, if it goes tense, if it goes to extra time, Uruguay plays like this is their natural habitat.

Uruguay is dangerous because they make you earn everything. They squeeze space. They chase loose balls like the ball owes them money. They spend zero energy being impressed by the stadium, the crowd, or the opponent's reputation. In a World Cup, where nerves can melt even great teams, Uruguay brings a strange calm. The kind that says, "We've been here before." That's why nobody circles Uruguay and thinks, easy. They circle Uruguay and think, brace yourself.

Bonus Trivia Quiz!

You think you are a true Uruguay fan? Try this bonus quiz!

1. In which city did football first take off fast in Uruguay, according to the book?

A) Salto
B) Montevideo
C) Maldonado
D) Colonia

2. What was one of the earliest recorded years a club match was played in Uruguay?

A) 1861
B) 1874
C) 1881
D) 1899

3. Which club is named in the book as being founded in 1891?

A) Nacional
B) Albion
C) Peñarol
D) Defensor

4. Uruguay won Olympic gold in 1924 in which city?

A) Paris
B) Rome
C) Berlin
D) Brussels

5. Uruguay won Olympic gold again in 1928 in which city?

A) Lisbon
B) London
C) Amsterdam
D) Zurich

6. Why does Uruguay's crest have four stars, as explained in the book?

A) Four stadiums they built
B) Four undefeated World Cups
C) Two Olympics (1924, 1928) and two World Cups (1930, 1950)
D) Four Copa América finals in a row

7. Which nickname belongs to Héctor Scarone?

A) El Jefe
B) El Príncipe
C) El Mago
D) El Pistolero

8. Which player's calm style inspired Zinedine Zidane so much he named his son after him?

A) Diego Forlán

B) Enzo Francescoli

C) Obdulio Varela

D) Héctor Scarone

9. Which striker is described as "babysitting a firework" in the book?

A) Edinson Cavani

B) Luis Suárez

C) Diego Forlán

D) Juan Alberto Schiaffino

10. What was the score of the 1930 World Cup final in Montevideo, according to the book?

A) Uruguay 1, Argentina 0

B) Uruguay 2, Argentina 1

C) Uruguay 3, Argentina 2

D) Uruguay 4, Argentina 2

11. to 1?

A) Alcides Ghiggia

B) Juan Alberto Schiaffino

C) Diego Forlán

D) Héctor Scarone

12. In 1950, after Ghiggia's goal, what did the Maracanã "do," according to the book?

A) Started singing louder
B) Threw fireworks
C) Went silent, like someone pressed mute on the stadium
D) Turned off the lights

13. What does "garra" mean in the phrase Garra Charrúa?

A) Crown
B) Claw
C) Song
D) Sky

14. What drink culture item is mentioned as something you might spot in the crowd?

A) Bubble tea
B) Hot chocolate
C) Mate
D) Lemonade

15. In 2010, which award did Diego Forlán win at the World Cup, according to the book?

A) Golden Boot
B) Golden Ball
C) Fair Play Award
D) Young Player Award

Super Fan Secret Challenge

Only a true Uruguay fan will know this.

(No Answer Provided)

- 163 -

Which opponent did Uruguay defeat in the 1950 match known as the Maracanazo?

A) Argentina

B) Brazil

C) Germany

D) Netherlands

Answer Key

1. B) Montevideo

2. C) 1881

3. B) Albion

4. A) Paris

5. C) Amsterdam

6. C) Two Olympics (1924, 1928) and two World Cups (1930, 1950)

7. C) El Mago

8. B) Enzo Francescoli

9. B) Luis Suárez

10. D) Uruguay 4, Argentina 2

11. B) Juan Alberto Schiaffino

12. C) Went silent, like someone pressed mute on the stadium

13. B) Claw

14. C) Mate

15. B) Golden Ball

Multi-Team Bonus Quiz!

Think you know all four teams in Group H? Try this ultimate group challenge!

1. Which country in Group H won the 2010 World Cup?

A) Uruguay
B) Spain
C) Saudi Arabia
D) Cape Verde

2. Cape Verde is made up of islands located in which ocean?

A) Pacific Ocean
B) Indian Ocean
C) Atlantic Ocean
D) Arctic Ocean

3. How many World Cups has Uruguay won?

A) 0
B) 1
C) 2
D) 3

4. Saudi Arabia's most famous World Cup upset came against which team in 2022?

A) Brazil
B) Germany
C) Argentina
D) France

5. What nickname is commonly used for Spain's national team?

A) La Roja
B) The Eagles
C) The Falcons
D) The Lions

6. Which country in Group H is making its first World Cup appearance?

A) Saudi Arabia
B) Uruguay
C) Spain
D) Cape Verde

7. Uruguay won their first World Cup in which year?

A) 1930
B) 1950
C) 1966
D) 1978

8. What is the capital city of Saudi Arabia?

A) Jeddah

B) Riyadh

C) Doha

D) Muscat

9. Spain's style of play is most known for what?

A) Long balls and speed

B) Physical strength

C) Possession and passing

D) Defensive counterattacks

10. Cape Verde reached the quarterfinals of which tournament in 2013 and 2023?

A) Copa America

B) Africa Cup of Nations

C) Asian Cup

D) Euros

11. Uruguay is located on which continent?

A) Europe

B) Africa

C) South America

D) Asia

12. Saudi Arabia's best World Cup finish came in which stage?

A) Group Stage
B) Round of 16
C) Quarterfinals
D) Semifinals

13. Which two Group H teams have played each other the most times historically?

A) Spain and Cape Verde
B) Saudi Arabia and Cape Verde
C) Spain and Uruguay
D) Uruguay and Cape Verde

14. Which Group H matchup has never been played before?

A) Spain vs Saudi Arabia
B) Uruguay vs Saudi Arabia
C) Spain vs Uruguay
D) Cape Verde vs Spain

15. Which Group H team has won multiple World Cups?

A) Spain
B) Saudi Arabia
C) Uruguay
D) Cape Verde

Multi-Team Answer Key

1. B) Spain

2. C) Atlantic Ocean

3. C) 2

4. C) Argentina

5. A) La Roja

6. D) Cape Verde

7. A) 1930

8. B) Riyadh

9. C) Possession and passing

10. B) Africa Cup of Nations

11. C) South America

12. B) Round of 16

13. C) Spain and Uruguay

14. D) Cape Verde vs Spain

15. C) Uruguay

WORLD CUP 2026 BRACKET

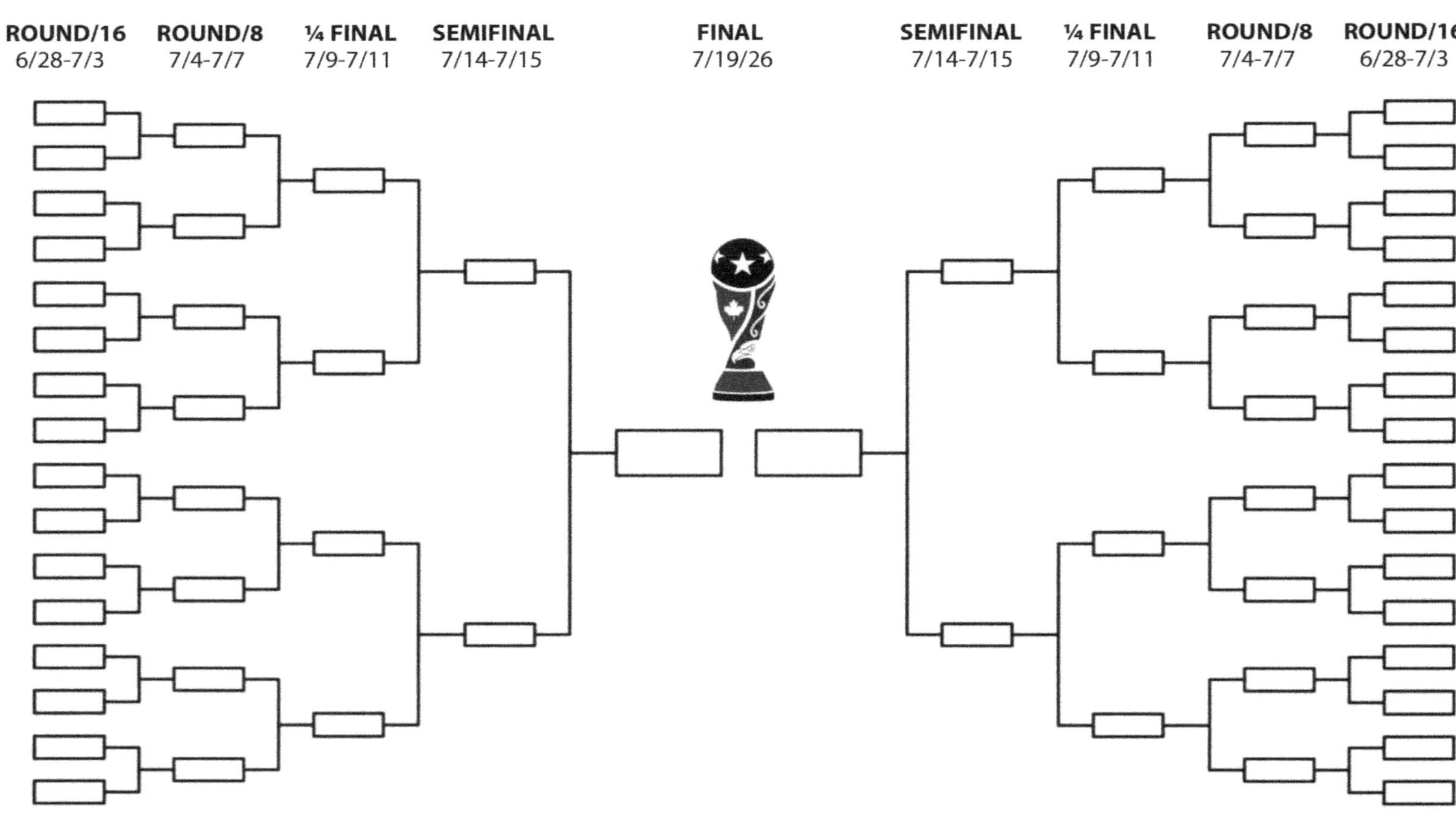

Be the Boss of Your Bracket

You have mastered the stats, met the legends, and scouted the rising stars. Now, it is time to step out of the stands and into the front office. On this page, you are not just a fan. You are a Head Coach, a Lead Scout, and a Fortune Teller all rolled into one.

This is not just a guide on how to watch the 2026 World Cup; it is your master plan for how to win it. With 48 teams descending on North America, the 2026 tournament will be the biggest and wildest in history. From the opening whistle to the final trophy lift, this bracket is your personal Command Center.

The Game Plan

1. Follow the Path: Start at the Round of 32. Use your expertise and decide who survives, who goes home.

2. Make the Call: Grab a pen and fill in the winners. Will a Dark Horse pull off a massive upset, or will heavyweights like Brazil and France dominate the pitch?

3. The Ultimate Glory: Trace your picks all the way to the middle. Who will be crowned World Champions under the lights at MetLife Stadium?

"Pro-Tip" House Rules: Want to be bold? Circle your biggest upset. That is your official "I saw it coming" pick to brag about later.

Choose Your Weapon: Use a pencil if you want to play it safe. Use a pen if you are fearless. Use a Sharpie if you live for the drama.

Fun Facts Wrap-Up

You made it through all four countries! You are officially a true Group H superfan! Now it is time to test your skills. Share these facts with your friends and see who knows their teams best!

Love the series?

Reviews help other fans discover Fun Fan Facts. If you enjoyed this book, we would really appreciate you sharing your thoughts and leaving a review.

Want more Fun Fan Facts?

Scan the QR code below to visit our site and explore bonus trivia, challenges, and special extras - including new teams, future series, and collectible fun as they are released.

Collect All the Fun Fan Facts Series!

Check off every book you read. See the full set on Amazon. Search "Fun Fan Facts Jake Liam."

World Cup 2026 Edition

- ☐ Algeria
- ☐ Argentina
- ☐ Australia
- ☐ Austria
- ☐ Belgium
- ☐ Brazil
- ☐ Canada
- ☐ Cape Verde
- ☐ Colombia
- ☐ Croatia
- ☐ Curaçao
- ☐ Ecuador
- ☐ Egypt
- ☐ England
- ☐ France
- ☐ Germany
- ☐ Ghana
- ☐ Haiti
- ☐ Iran
- ☐ Ivory Coast
- ☐ Japan
- ☐ Jordan
- ☐ Mexico
- ☐ Morocco
- ☐ Netherlands
- ☐ New Zealand
- ☐ Norway
- ☐ Panama
- ☐ Paraguay
- ☐ Portugal
- ☐ Qatar
- ☐ Saudi Arabia
- ☐ Scotland
- ☐ Senegal
- ☐ South Africa
- ☐ South Korea
- ☐ Spain
- ☐ Switzerland
- ☐ Tunisia
- ☐ United States
- ☐ Uruguay
- ☐ Uzbekistan

World Cup 2026 Group Edition

- ☐ Group A
- ☐ Group B
- ☐ Group C
- ☐ Group D
- ☐ Group E
- ☐ Group F
- ☐ Group G
- ☐ Group H
- ☐ Group I
- ☐ Group J
- ☐ Group K
- ☐ Group L

English Football Edition

☐ Arsenal F.C.

☐ Aston Villa F.C.

☐ Chelsea F.C.

☐ Everton F.C.

☐ Fulham F.C.

☐ Liverpool F.C.

☐ Manchester City

☐ Manchester United

☐ Newcastle United F.C.

☐ Tottenham Hotspur

☐ West Ham United

☐ Wrexham A.F.C.

NBA Edition

☐ Atlanta Hawks

☐ Boston Celtics

☐ Brooklyn Nets

☐ Charlotte Hornets

☐ Chicago Bulls

☐ Cleveland Cavaliers

☐ Dallas Mavericks

☐ Denver Nuggets

☐ Detroit Pistons

☐ Golden State Warriors

☐ Houston Rockets

☐ Indiana Pacers

☐ LA Clippers

☐ Los Angeles Lakers

☐ Memphis Grizzlies

☐ Miami Heat

☐ Milwaukee Bucks

☐ Minnesota Timberwolves

☐ New Orleans Pelicans

☐ New York Knicks

☐ Oklahoma City Thunder

☐ Orlando Magic

☐ Philadelphia 76ers

☐ Phoenix Suns

☐ Portland Trail Blazers

☐ Sacramento Kings

☐ San Antonio Spurs

☐ Toronto Raptors

☐ Utah Jazz

☐ Washington Wizards

About the Author

Jake is a 13-year-old sports fan who loves football, American football, and basketball. He plays soccer as a goalie and dreams of one day playing for West Ham United and helping teach kids to love the game. His passion for sports runs in the family - his dad was a professional baseball player, and his stepdad sparked his love for West Ham. Through the Fun Fan Facts series, he shares the fun and excitement of sports with fans everywhere.

9 781972 300374